PR
HACKING SC

MW00487734

Hacking School Libraries is a fun take on how to transform your program into an immersive learning experience for all students. Filled with practical ideas by incredible practitioners, this handbook makes it easy to inspire change using many of the resources that you already have. It's not your grandparents' school library anymore!
ADAM BELLOW, CO-FOUNDER, BREAKOUT EDU

Hacking School Libraries offers specific strategies, supported by thoughtful rationales, for upgrading your school library into a thriving, current program and space. Early career librarians and veterans alike will find solutions and inspiration in the tips, lessons learned, and stories shared by authors Kristina Holzweiss and Stony Evans, with additional reflections culled from creative, respected school librarians representing a range of schools and grade levels.
REBECCA J. MORRIS, SCHOOL LIBRARY CONNECTION

Authors Kristina Holzweiss and Stony Evans are two of the most respected thought leaders and practitioners in the school library field. Their book, *Hacking School Libraries*, is an essential resource for any modern-day library media specialist. It is filled with actionable tips and strategies that anyone can easily implement tomorrow.
LAURA FLEMING, LIBRARY MEDIA SPECIALIST, AUTHOR OF *WORLDS OF MAKING* AND *THE KICKSTART GUIDE TO MAKING GREAT MAKERSPACES*

I love the Hack Learning books, and this new book, *Hacking School Libraries*, fits perfectly into the series. This book is an indispensable resource for all librarians, and also the administrators who support them. Kristina and Stony offer up incredible, easy-to-follow hacks for any grade-level library! I can't wait to implement some of them in my library!

ELISSA MALESPINA, TEACHER-LIBRARIAN,
ISTE LIBRARIANS NETWORK PAST PRESIDENT

Hacking your library by adding a makerspace can seem like a daunting task, but *Hacking School Libraries* is the guide that makes integrating spaces and the culture of making an easy-to-implement process. Here, you will find useful tips and tricks designed through years of experience in the space to start creating a makerspace program tomorrow.

NICHOLAS PROVENZANO, MAKERSPACE DIRECTOR
AND AUTHOR OF *YOUR STARTER GUIDE TO MAKERSPACES*
AND *THE MAKER MENTALITY*

I really like the quick reading style and the focus banners for each hack. This is a very useful guide for new school library professionals or those thirsting for easy, practical, and inexpensive ideas to revitalize their school libraries. My highest praise is that it's written by practitioners FOR practitioners.

DR. BEA BAADEN, DIRECTOR OF THE SCHOOL LIBRARY PROGRAM,
PALMER SCHOOL OF LIBRARY AND INFORMATION SCIENCE,
LONG ISLAND UNIVERSITY

When I learned that Kristina and Stony were writing a book to fit into one of my favorite series, I was so excited and couldn't think of a better duo to do so! School librarians will find *Hacking School Libraries* such an amazing read and resource in so many ways. The hacks found in this book are terrific for any grade level and will help guide librarians to make a difference in their library, school, and community!

SHANNON MCCLINTOCK MILLER, TEACHER-LIBRARIAN IN VAN METER, IOWA; FUTURE READY LIBRARIAN SPOKESPERSON, IOWA

Hacking School Libraries is a gem! Even as a non-librarian, I am finding actionable steps that I can use in my own practice. The hacks are solid, and the authors even include ways to overcome pushback. They also highlight the work of other school librarians so that readers can visualize these hacks in action.

SARAH THOMAS, FOUNDER, EDUMATCH

Hacking School Libraries is the practical book that I have been waiting for a teacher-librarian to publish! This is the book I will be recommending to school librarians who want constructive and attainable suggestions on how to not only transform their library space, but also their library practices and in turn, their school. The stories and ideas from Stony, Kristina, and other respected colleagues in the school library world spotlight tried-and-true practices that have transformed school library programs across the nation.

SHERRY GICK, DIRECTOR OF INNOVATIVE LEARNING—FIVE STAR TECHNOLOGY SOLUTIONS, TEACHER-LIBRARIAN, 2015 LJ MOVER & SHAKER

HACKING
SCHOOL LIBRARIES

HACKING
SCHOOL LIBRARIES

10 Ways to Incorporate Library Media
Centers into Your Learning Community

HACK
Learning
SERIES

KRISTINA A. HOLZWEISS
STONY EVANS

Published by Times 10
Highland Heights, OH
Times10Books.com

Cover Design by Najdan Mancic
Interior Design by Steven Plummer
Editing by Carrie White-Parrish
Proofreading by Jennifer Jas

Library of Congress Cataloging-in-Publication Data is available.
ISBN: 978-1-948212-06-9
First Printing: August, 2018

CONTENTS

✱ beginning librarian start here
✓ experienced librarian - start here + add
each year

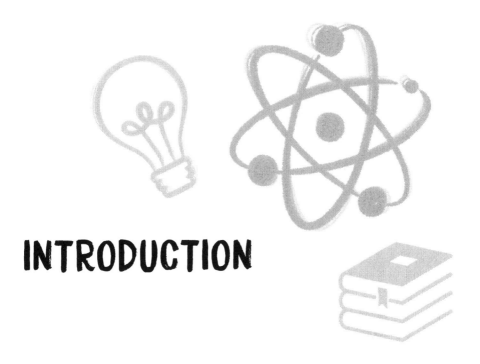

INTRODUCTION

Y ou are reading a book filled with hacks—the kind of book that we wish we had when we first became librarians. Here you will find ways to promote reading, secure funding, connect with reluctant readers through makerspaces, redesign the library environment, and develop a program that works for you and your students. We hope these ideas inspire you wherever you are in your journey, whether you're just setting out, developing, or nearing the end of your career. Change your school's vision of what a library is. Make yours the library that your students will remember and talk about.

Libraries have always been a place for both of us to connect with books and knowledge. As young children, we frequented our school and public libraries for their reading programs, and the library staff began to welcome us by our names. When we grew older, libraries became places where we could access resources for our research projects and use the computers. Even though we pursued other careers in education (Kristina was an English teacher and Stony was a music teacher), we eventually returned to our primary passions and became school librarians. We agree that it was the best career choice we have ever made!

Fast forward to 2018, and the perception of a library has drastically changed. School libraries are places where you can find not only books but also audiobooks, ebooks, and Chromebooks. They are places where students can create green screen movies, design video games, develop computational skills and 3D print prototypes, and make noise. They are places where students are empowered to share their voices, be independent thinkers, and participate in the global digital community. They are places where students are preparing for the future today.

They are also welcoming places of refuge, and places to call home.

The potential for change in the school library is limitless. In the following pages, you will find transformative tips that will help you make your program an essential part of the learning community. This book follows the format of other books in the Hack Learning Series. Each chapter presents easy-to-follow strategies under these section headings: The Problem, The Hack, What You Can Do Tomorrow, A Blueprint for Full Implementation, Overcoming Pushback, and The Hack in Action.

As you begin your journey using our library hacks, you will meet other passionate educators who will challenge you to improve for those you serve. We know you will find this adventure life-changing. Most important, your students will be changed as you start *Hacking School Libraries*.

HACK 1
TRANSFORM THE SPACE
Build it and they will come

It was good to walk into a library again; it smelled like home.

— Elizabeth Kostova, Author

THE PROBLEM: LIBRARIES AREN'T DESIGNED WITH FORM AND FUNCTION—OR AS WELCOMING PLACES

For most of the school day, students sit in seats arranged in rows. Our parents, grandparents, and great-grandparents sat in rows, so this is something that we can all relate to. Those students sit beneath fluorescent lights, in silence, facing the front of the room—just like we all did when we were young. The problem is that this means those classrooms are set up more like factory floors than think tanks.

The rooms in our homes, on the other hand, are arranged for different purposes. A table in a dining room allows family members to join together and face each other for interaction during their daily meals. In the living room, various sizes of seating options allow for conversation, while also giving most of the people a direct view of the television. Bedroom furniture provides storage for clothes, as well as a place to rest from a day of work.

Libraries need to take their cues from the way a house is set up. Instead of sticking to the same old thing, libraries should be designed to serve multiple purposes during the school day, for both students and teachers. If librarians miss that point and fail to arrange a physical environment that can accommodate a variety of tasks, they'll see one result: The library will be underused. An organized, welcoming, and user-friendly space, however, will help patrons develop positive feelings about visiting the library. It will go from being the boring domain of a "bunhead" to a more dynamic place where patrons are invited to read, explore, connect, collaborate, share, and create.

It all starts with designing a library that has form and function— and invites its visitors to stretch and create, rather than conform to old ideas.

THE HACK: TRANSFORM THE SPACE

Look at the library space through the lens of your students, your colleagues, your administrators, and even your students' parents. Is it a place where people feel welcome and inspired to explore and research? Is it user-friendly, and are resources accessible to everyone? Does the environment foster growth and independence in a nurturing atmosphere? If the answer to any of those questions is no, then you have the start of your problem. Luckily, you also have the start of your journey.

FOCUS ON THE AREAS THAT ARE THE OLDEST FIRST, AS THOSE ARE THE ONES THAT NEED THE MOST ATTENTION.... DO YOU REALLY NEED A BOOK ABOUT SPACE WRITTEN BEFORE THE ASTRONAUTS LANDED ON THE MOON? YOU ARE A SCHOOL LIBRARIAN, NOT AN ARCHIVIST.

Take a lesson from Starbucks and the Apple store, both places where people gather for an experience, rather than just to make a purchase. Like them, a library is in the business of satisfying the needs of a variety of customers. So you need to start by considering the customers if you're going to attract them. If you work to create an environment that allows students to learn the way they want to learn, this tells them that you respect them and want to include them in the library's programs. You've designed the entire library for that specific purpose! When you care enough about interior design and functionality to make it all about the students, it says that you care about them and their learning.

Just like adults, kids want to go where everybody knows their names and seems glad they came. Just imagine how excited your students will be when they realize that you're redesigning your library with them in mind—and making it both easier and more attractive to get involved. That excitement will translate into participation and traffic.

This might sound overwhelming and scary, but remember that a library transformation doesn't have to mean a full remodel. Many smaller changes can still translate into a large impact. Simple, creative facelifts to layout and décor, which focus on form and function, can help increase productivity. The trick is to start with who your students are, and build or decorate for them.

WHAT YOU CAN DO TOMORROW

- **Weed.** Why are you holding onto books that are outdated, inappropriate, or damaged? This sticks you right into that old-fashioned, no-longer-relevant teaching column. Upload your collection and analyze it through your circulation software to determine the average age of the entire collection and the average age of each section. Then start to figure out how you can change it up. Focus on the areas that are the oldest first, as those are the ones that need the most attention. We all hope that we will fit into our old clothes at the back of the closet, but do you really need a book about space written before the astronauts landed on the moon? You are a school librarian, not an archivist.

- **Declutter.** Do your patrons suffer from sensory overload when they enter the library? Clean it up and simplify to immediately and easily update the space. Remove or modify signs and displays. Create a short list of positive expectations, rather than the list of "do-nots." Ditch your desk, which is old-fashioned and taking up valuable floor space that could be used for a reading nook or collaborative workspace. Attach anti-slip tape to the bottoms of bookends to keep books in place, use paint stirrers as shelf markers, and place baskets on the floor for students to return books that need to be reshelved. Rubber refrigerator door liners will keep books from slipping on carts. All of this will clean up the space and make it easier and more pleasant for students.

- **Organize.** Many of the following suggestions are based on libraries for the younger grades, but can be adapted for the ages of your learners. Create a cubby system where students can store their belongings so they don't have to worry about keeping track of things while they're browsing or working. Scrapbooking storage boxes are the perfect size for makerspace or literacy kits. Hang curtains from spring tension rods to hide supplies, and use hanging shoe organizers for pens, highlighters, markers, scissors, and crayons. Numbered and color-coded baskets make it easy to distribute supplies. Utilize mobile, lockable charging carts to keep track of and organize any technological devices you have in the space. Use clothing racks to hang posters and charts so they remain straight and protected, and use PVC pipe to create a storage system for headphones. Purchase a personal laminator to create long-lasting, color-coded labels. Create signage that is visually appealing and clear, and use both text and images to make it easier for all students, especially English language learners and special education students, to understand what you're asking of them.

- **Add color.** Embrace color, but be sure to choose a complementary palette appropriate for the ages of your students. Experiment with functional paint (magnetic paint, chalkboard paint, or dry-erase) to transform tables, cabinets, walls, and even your circulation counter into brainstorming canvases. Paint a wall green for an instant green screen without taking up additional space. For temporary art, use Post-it notes or paint sample chips from your local hardware store. If your school is able to afford new carpeting, opt for carpet squares and use different colors and patterns in the squares to delineate specific zones. It is much easier and cheaper to replace one square rather than the entire carpet. Use large rugs if you are on a budget. Reupholster furniture with a staple gun to update the look and bring more color and fun into the library.

- **Decorate.** Display student-created art on the tops of your bookcases, and invite your students to design book carts, reading chairs, murals, or even ceiling tiles. Jazz up bookshelves with contact paper. Use Command hooks, Velcro, or hot glue over painter's tape to instantly hang and attach décor without creating holes in your walls. Live plants help to soften sharp visual corners, add oxygen to the environment, and offer students opportunities to care for and learn about horticulture—and it all makes the library a friendlier, more approachable place.

A BLUEPRINT FOR FULL IMPLEMENTATION

Step 1: Assess.

Step back and take an objective look at the entire library space, as well as each section (fiction, nonfiction, reference) individually. Walk through the library, taking pictures and videos for reflection. Use the Google Cardboard app to create a 360-degree panorama for a better picture, and then make a list of what has been working well and what you would like to improve. Take note of architectural elements such as windows, brick walls, doors, and pillars that may challenge your designs, and start thinking about how you can use them. Observe the "flow" of people entering and exiting and how they use the space.

Consider the technology that you already have, as well as technology that your district may purchase in the future, and what you could use most efficiently. It is easier to move a mobile cart of iPads, Chromebooks, and laptops than it is to create a computer lab, for instance. Speak to your administrators about their vision for not only technology but also the Wi-Fi infrastructure to support it. Allow your mind to start building your plan based on the needs you see.

OFFER RELEVANT DATA TO BACK UP YOUR CLAIM THAT A LIBRARY TRANSFORMATION WILL INCREASE PATRON VISITS AND CIRCULATION NUMBERS—WHICH, IN TURN, WILL RAISE READING SCORES.

Step 2: Seek feedback.

Create a paper or digital survey to find out what your students and colleagues are thinking. What do they like about the space? What *don't* they like? Ask why. Browse through magazines, catalogs, blogs, websites, social media, and Pinterest, and share pictures of ideas that you like, and ideas that you *don't* like, with your test audience. Remember to ask for input from special education teachers, who can share the physical needs of their students and how the library can best accommodate them.

Once you have looked at the space through an objective lens, speak to a library furniture company representative. Then create a library design committee comprised of students, teachers, parents, and administrators for their input. Present what you have discovered through your assessment, and invite others to express their opinions about the usability of the library space. Share stories about successful library transformations, and include the positive impact those transformations had on the school learning community. Offer relevant data to back up your claim that a library transformation will increase patron visits and circulation numbers—which, in turn, will raise reading scores.

Step 3: Change the layout.

Consider the precepts of Universal Design when you're deciding how furniture, lighting, and layout can help all students to learn and succeed. Whether you are planning a facelift or a full remodel, aim for open, flexible, collaborative spaces with access to power, multipurpose storage, and furniture. Many librarians don't have the luxury of knocking down walls or adding skylights, but you can make sure that you use every space to its best possible purpose. Use painter's tape to mark off the placement of furniture before you move it, to make sure that the pieces will fit and will allow patrons to move freely. Put casters on bookcases and cabinets. Consider how the furniture you already have can help define and create open areas for various functions such as a reading lounge, a classroom, and a makerspace. For example, a high metal cabinet can serve as a section divider, storage for a makerspace, a Lego wall, or a message center. Just attach strong magnets to the back of Lego baseplates, and place where needed.

Image 1.1: Removable Lego baseplates increase functionality.

Image 1.2: A metal cabinet offers much-needed storage space.

Step 4: Consider a variety of seating options.

Notice recent trends regarding flexible seating and "double duty" furniture, and you'll see there is a lot to take advantage of. Visit the carpet store and ask for square samples. Create a yoga ball chair base by forming a circle with a pool noodle and securing the ends with colorful duct tape. Sew cushions and put them on top of plastic milk crate cartons, and you will have seating as well as storage.

Put under-the-table portable cycle pedalers in certain spots to help fidgety students burn up their energy. Other options include exercise bikes, portable ellipticals, stand-up desks, and rocking chairs. A few beanbag chairs won't break the bank, and yoga mats are a comfortable, durable alternative to sitting on a hard floor. Turn large plastic buckets upside down, and add cushions (outdoor patio furniture cushions are larger and more durable than floor pillows). Use flip tables as collaborative workspaces, zone dividers, and brainstorming boards, and extend your circulation counter with height-adjustable hospital tray tables, so your students can sit at bar stools and enjoy your company without compromising your work area. Create a flexible space in which you can incorporate new ideas without restructuring.

Image 1.3: A reading lounge or book nook is a cozy space to curl up with a good book.

Image 1.4: Bright-colored plastic chairs make clean-up easy in makerspaces.

Image 1.5: Adjustable hospital tray tables serve double-duty for standing or sitting.

Step 5: Draft a budget and seek funding.

Have your team help you create a planning chart. Determine the goals that you would like to achieve, and what you will need to achieve them. Create a list of priorities, the cost of each change, and how long it will take to implement. Pay close attention to which changes can be performed without prior permission from your building or district administrators. Requests for lighting, additional outlets, and Wi-Fi hubs will definitely require conversations with your supervisors. When you speak with them, have a Plan A, Plan B, and Plan C in place so you are prepared to pitch changes within a variety of budget ranges.

Try to match potential donors and funding sources with each possible change. Is there a local company that will give your school a discount on furniture, or a carpet store that has a sale on particular colors or styles of carpeting? Write grants that demonstrate how a library transformation will impact student learning. Present your pitch with photos and interviews to your parent association and school board for their support.

Step 6: Document the transformation.

Create an online public album that includes pictures and videos of each step of the transformation. These will help you to assess the changes that you make, and inspire a community experience. Students, parents, teachers, community members, and other stakeholders will appreciate being able to experience the transformation virtually. These records will also be helpful for other librarians in your district as they advocate for transformations in their own libraries.

Step 7: Celebrate.

When the transformation is complete—celebrate! Work with your students to create invitations and decorations for the big reveal, and invite teachers to participate in the celebration by supporting their students and supplying snacks and music. Invite your superintendent and administrators, the school board, your principal, and parents to enjoy the new space together for the first time. Organize student guides to take guests on tours through the library, explaining the transformation process and their opinions. Show appreciation to the custodians who helped you move your furniture by hosting a luncheon for them, too, and send them a written thank-you note, with a copy sent to the principal.

OVERCOMING PUSHBACK

The library is one of the largest and most used classrooms in the school, and is frequently visited by a variety of people. Each person has his or her own preconceived notions of what a library should look like, based on past experiences, and while some people will embrace change, others will be frightened by it. It is up to you to help make your students and faculty feel comfortable (and even excited) about the library transformation. Following are some of the questions you might get—and the answers you should have ready.

This doesn't look like our old library. Whether positive or negative, people often have a visceral reaction to change. Some may become upset about seeing you weed out certain older books, while others may disapprove of the new layout or color scheme. But you have done your research and consulted with your team, and you made the changes for a reason. Allow people the time to become acclimated to the library transformation, and collect data about circulation and attendance, as well as anecdotes. It will be difficult to argue with your evidence.

We don't have the money for a full remodel. This could be true, but it doesn't mean it should stop you from updating the space. Make small changes that cost little to no money, and refuse to back down about your needs. People are more willing to donate or "find money in another budget code" once they see that you mean business. Rather than throwing up your hands in despair, do what you can with what you have, and keep working toward finding more money or supplies. Your school might not have the money, but that doesn't mean your students don't deserve the best effort possible.

We have books and a librarian. That's all we need. Explain that the library, as well as the entire school, is a place to prepare students today for the challenges of tomorrow. Noam Chomsky said, "If you're teaching today what you were teaching five years ago, either the field is dead or you are." Cite statistics from the Pew Research Center regarding our changing society and technology use. Share the American Association of School Librarians (AASL) National School Library Standards for Learners, School Librarians, and School Libraries. Also share the International Society for Technology in Education (ISTE) Standards for Students, and the Future Ready Schools Framework. The library should be addressing these needs—and failing to do so is a failure for your students.

THE HACK IN ACTION

Katie's Story

Katie Darty is one of two librarians at North Buncombe High School in Weaverville, North Carolina. With little more than $600, Katie was determined to transform her library with her colleague Cindy Mackiernan. Katie says, "When Cindy and I first hatched the idea of remodeling our library, it seemed like an impossible task. We soon realized that we didn't have to do it alone." The school's interior design teacher, Stephanie Griffin, put the librarians in touch with students interested in helping with the remodel, other departments within the school, and even various businesses in and around the community that could provide discounts or donated materials.

Students of the Career and Technical Education Program participated in the design thinking process to help create solutions for the library, the welding class transformed the library's old metal bookshelves into a new magazine rack, the carpentry class sanded all of the tables for painting, the interior design class painted the tabletops, and the art department painted murals on the wall and art on the wooden chairs. "Paint can go a long way to help change for form and for function," Katie says. In the end, Katie's library was the product of a group effort.

Todd's Story

Todd Burleson, 2016 School Librarian of the Year, of Hubbard Woods School in Winnetka, Illinois, transformed his library into a playground of learning. First, Todd visited a number of libraries in the greater Chicago area and, with those places in mind, in addition to images of libraries from around the world, he began making his wish list. Next, he considered the space as a blank slate. He made a digital template in Google Drawings to prototype efficiently and quickly, over and over, and then printed the basic template on a large poster printer so that he had a physical way to prototype spaces and layouts.

To save funds and resources, Todd transformed existing structures. He cut the bookcases apart and reinforced the tops and bottoms. He purchased bulk industrial casters so he could put everything on wheels. As a substitute for whiteboard, Todd purchased shower board, an inexpensive covering for shower stalls that is essentially medium-density fiberboard with a melamine coating on it. For the cost of one whiteboard, Todd was able to cover an entire hallway with shower board. Then he modified the old computer lab surfaces by using industrial plumbing pipe and fixtures to add strength and rigidity to the old countertops. For under $200, he created a woodworking surface, coding area, and sewing station.

SUMMARY

Breaking down your library can be an intimidating task, but it is also an opportunity to rebuild it into an exciting place where your students will enjoy visiting. Libraries serve not only as classrooms but also as learning commons for the entire school community. When you take the time to consider how the library is really used, you can redesign it in ways that increase the number of programs and make them more efficient. Time is a nonrenewable resource, but when we create organized environments, we can spend more time on teaching and building relationships.

HACK 2
SHAKE UP THOSE POLICIES, PROCEDURES, AND PROTOCOLS
Focus on what matters: the students

Customers don't measure you on how hard you tried, they measure you on what you deliver.

— STEVE JOBS, INNOVATOR

THE PROBLEM: LIBRARIANS SERVE MANY ROLES, WITH RESPONSIBILITIES VYING FOR PRIORITY

MANY PEOPLE DON'T know exactly what school librarians do. Your administrators don't know, your teachers don't know, your students don't know ... not even your family and friends know. And when you were studying library science in college, you THOUGHT you knew.

School librarians are managers of programs, paper, and most important—people. But sometimes the housekeeping aspects of libraries get in the way of teaching, which is what we are initially hired to do. Librarians are masters of multitasking… setting, stirring, and watching proverbial pots of boiling water on a stove. Some of us are fortunate to co-teach with another librarian or to have a staff. Many, or maybe even most, of us do not.

At the end of the day, there will always be books to shelve, lessons to write, and classes to schedule. The key is to create systems that are time-saving, meaningful, and fair to our students.

THE HACK: SHAKE UP THOSE POLICIES, PROCEDURES, AND PROTOCOLS

Are you new to your position and afraid to rock the boat with your administrators and faculty? Have you inherited policies that you don't agree with? Or are you a veteran librarian who has had the same procedures in place for the past twenty years? Now is the time to consider how to transform your library program for today's students—regardless of how new you are in your job, or how things were done before. Gone are the days of "sit down and shush." Today's libraries are vibrant places of learning where we need to encourage students to share their voices, while also creating collaborative connections with faculty and administrators.

Let's start with the tried-and-true statement of "Yes, but." Think about it: When you interact with patrons, are you using yes to say no? "Yes, but you are only allowed to take out two books at a time." "Yes, but the library is closed after school." "Yes, but you need to know how the Dewey Decimal System works before you can borrow a book." Let's get rid of that old way of thinking and move forward into something more helpful. Take a moment to consider using "Yes, and" to open the conversation instead, and go from there. Where else can you change things up so that they work better for both you and the students? Create *new* policies and procedures to provide the structure you need, while also making the library a welcoming place for all.

A LIBRARY IS NOT JUST A PLACE, IT IS A SERVICE—AND STUDENTS ARE OUR CUSTOMERS. THE BETTER THE EXPERIENCE THEY HAVE, THE MORE LIKELY THEY ARE TO VISIT AGAIN.

WHAT YOU CAN DO TOMORROW

- **Create a mission statement.** Write a mission statement for your library that reflects what is most important to you and your school community. A mission statement is your library's purpose, and it serves as a guide for decision-making. With this mission statement in mind, you will be able to develop a clear direction for the library program. This mission conveys to your key stakeholders what to expect from you, and what the benefits of the library are. A mission statement posted in a prominent place is a public acknowledgment of the library's importance in the school environment, and the role of the school librarian. It can also serve as a springboard for productive conversations.

- **End overdue fines.** Assess policies such as overdue fines and limits on the number of books that students may borrow. Are there legitimate reasons to continue these policies? If not, stop tracking nickels and dimes for books that students fail to turn in on time. Instead, email them or print out reminders if someone else needs those overdue titles. These books can be quickly renewed or returned without a big fuss. Have students pay only for lost or damaged materials, or find a replacement at a local bookstore so you won't have to wait for a book order. If a student can't pay for a book, have him or her "work off" the cost through reading a certain number of minutes or by peer tutoring.

- **Build your schedule using an online calendar.** Whether your library runs a fixed or a flexible schedule, use an online calendar to document your library activity for the school year. Show what you have coming up, and use it to advocate for more resources, including staffing. Use this as a record of closures due to testing or administrative meetings when you're scheduling library accessibility. People can access online calendars easily, anywhere and anytime, so share your calendar on your website or through email. If administration and secretaries have access to your calendar, they can easily reach a class in an emergency.

- **Communicate with your students and their parents.** A library is not just a place, it is a service—and students are our customers. The better the experience they have, the more likely they are to visit again. Use the Remind or Bloomz app to share age-appropriate information with your students, such as reminders about book return dates, new books in the library, research paper due dates, event announcements, and trivia questions for contests.

Communicating during the summer months and vacations is a fantastic way to encourage reading.

- **Be sensitive to differences.** Our world has become more diverse with respect to culture, religion, gender, language, and economics. Be mindful of our differences. For example, during the Holy Month of Ramadan, Muslims must fast from sunrise to sunset. Because of this, some of your students may feel uncomfortable remaining in the cafeteria during their lunch period. The library may serve as an alternative placement for students who need a place of refuge. Use gender-neutral language (students, scholars, everyone, children, Mr. or Mrs. Smith's class) when speaking and referring to students. Avoid categorizing (such as by boys or girls). Instead, group students by what color they are wearing, their birthdays, or the alphabet. Be inclusive and take everyone into account to make sure all feel welcome, and they'll come to think of the library as a refuge.

Here we. . .

- are respectful, supportive, and kind.
- encourage one another to do our best.
- cooperate and collaborate.
- develop 21st century skills.
- pursue our own interests.
- participate in the global community.
- practice proper digital citizenship.
- apply knowledge to real-world situations.
- participate in community service projects.
- learn through hands-on activities.
- celebrate each other's accomplishments.
- take proper care of resources.
- can share ideas and ask questions.

Image 2.1: A mission statement posted in a prominent location demonstrates the focus of a school library.

A BLUEPRINT FOR FULL IMPLEMENTATION

Step 1: Make orientation memorable.

One of the most important things a school librarian can do is to have an exciting library orientation for new students and their parents—even if libraries didn't do this in the past. Make the experience interactive with a Breakout EDU game. Create puzzles for students to solve by using library resources and services. For instance, offer a simple puzzle based on the library hours as a game for classes to compete to solve. With each solved puzzle, new users learn about library services and procedures. Breakout EDU is a great way to teach library skills to new students or to introduce the library to parents on an open house night, and it builds new processes for the library.

Image 2.2: Breakout EDU experiences promote collaboration and problem-solving.

Step 2: Create a dynamic website.

In our opinion, nothing is worse than visiting a school website and not seeing a library online presence. A website is a launch pad—a resource for the entire learning community—but it is too often ignored. Popular website creators for school libraries are LibGuides, Weebly, Wix, Google Sites, and Adobe Spark. School library websites should be updated as necessary to accommodate the growing needs of teachers and students. Topics you may want to include are a mission statement, library rules and policies, and an email address and other contact information. Include links to digital resources (online catalog, databases, ebooks), a research handbook, pages for school projects or pathfinders, links to the public library and other community organizations, and screencast tutorials. Share weekly or monthly news, favorite apps and web tools, makerspace information, book recommendations and trailers, and links to author tutorials. These resources will encourage your students to visit the library. Post a scheduling calendar and a teacher collaboration needs assessment form for the teachers.

Adding cool features to your website can build the "wow" factor. Consider adding interactivity using the ThingLink app to tag camera images, or use the TouchCast app to create smart videos and share any file. Use the enhanced Teleport 360 Editor app to create interactive 360 stories. Add the SpeakPipe widget to your website so your visitors can leave you voice messages. Just imagine how they'll react when you reply back with the answers to their questions! Create tutorials to access the databases and ebooks using the Screencast-O-Matic web tool. You can upload the videos to your website, and share the links with your faculty. Even better, hosting these on your website will free you up to do other things in the library.

Step 3: Run a well-oiled machine.

The more engaged students are, the more smoothly your library program will run. If you have a flexible schedule, record student visits with a sign-in book or through a Google Form. You will be able to transform these statistics into an infographic for your annual report. As adults, it is our responsibility to serve as role models for children. A sign posted at the library entrance and sharing prompts for manners will remind your students to say "hello," "please," and "thank you." Instead of raising your voice, clap your hands, play some chimes, or briefly beat a tambourine. You can also use a simple bell, or invest in a wireless door chime. Set up a self-checkout station. Your students will learn independence and enjoy having the "power" to circulate their own books. It will also take this responsibility off *your* shoulders.

As an incentive to return books on time, distribute punch cards to your students. When your students have a designated number of punches, stickers, or stamps, give them a small prize. Gamify classroom management with ClassDojo or Classcraft so that your students take ownership of their behaviors and see a correlation between their choices and their successes. Create a moment for your students by establishing a milestone ritual in your library. When your students ask you to sign their yearbooks, ask them to leave *their* mark on the library rocking chair, a book cart, or your desk blotter. That item will become your most prized possession when you retire, and the action will help them invest in the library itself.

Step 4: Assess student learning.

Assessments may take place before, during, or after a lesson. Use simple assessments like paper exit tickets written in the form of emails, texts, or tweets, or let students use dry-erase boards, or hold up signs that say *yes/true, no/false,* or *I'm ok/I need help.* For an online version of an exit ticket, consider allowing students to respond on a Padlet or a Flipgrid. They can also document their learning using the Seesaw app. Other options include Kahoot, Quizizz, Quizlet, Quizalize, Nearpod, Socrative, and Plickers. These assessments will tell you what the students think of the library and its programs and will help you to improve and streamline them.

YOUR GOAL IS TO PROMOTE THE LIBRARY AND MAKE IT MORE USER-FRIENDLY FOR YOUR LEARNING COMMUNITY— NOT TO ADHERE TO OLD RULES.

Step 5: Extend library hours.

Some families haven't developed meaningful connections with library culture, and part of the problem is that they can't get to the library within the restricted traditional hours. Work with your administration so you can offer extended hours one day each month for those families to visit your library. Offer these hours during conference days or meetings, when parents will be visiting the school anyway. During this time, provide opportunities for students and their families to use the computers and check out books. Students can also use that time to teach technology skills to the adults in their families.

Ask members of the honor society to supervise students' younger siblings. Create a family collection of resources about parenting, career exploration, and college information, and host special family game nights and parent-child book clubs. Invite college students to help high school seniors write their application essays. Show parents how they can access the online databases at home. To prevent the "summer slide," allow students to take home books to enjoy during their vacation. Give all of those bags you receive during conferences to your students, so they can carry their treasures home. Open the library once or twice during the summer so your students can exchange their books. You'll be reaching students you were never able to reach before, just by bending a few of the old-fashioned rules.

OVERCOMING PUSHBACK

If you begin changing traditional policies that teachers and administrators have been accustomed to for years, expect some pushback. The following comments are likely to be delivered to you soon after word gets out. Remember, your goal is to promote the library and make it more user-friendly for your learning community—not to adhere to old rules.

Overdue fines teach students responsibility. Overdue fines just punish learners for forgetting to renew or return a book, and often keep students from borrowing additional books when they cannot pay the fine. Overdue fines promote a negative view of the library. Find other ways to remind students to return materials, and promote reading by keeping book circulation moving. It's more important to get readers to return, not the books to return. Only charge for missing or damaged items.

"Library" is not a core class, so why would parents want to learn about it? The library is not a core class, but it should be the hub of the learning community. We need parents as supporters of our school library programs, and to do this, we must inform and educate them about the many resources in the library. Parents are important stakeholders in the school, and we must advocate by inviting them into our spaces.

The library only interests a small part of the student population. If this is true, it must change. The library is for everyone, and if the student population is not interested in the library, it is a failing school program. Get out in the hallways to advertise. Get the students interested in books, innovation, and technology. It is a school librarian's mission to shatter the idea that the library is only for a small portion of the student population.

THE HACK IN ACTION

Kristina's Story

After twenty-three years of teaching, I have finally found a way to clone myself; a way to extend my teaching to other classrooms and even homes. Google Classroom is my secret weapon. This year, instead of simply posting information on our library website, I created a Research Tools Google Classroom. As we write this, 850 students, more than half of our student population, are members. When I teach information literacy lessons, each student has his or her own copy of my documents to modify. This makes the lessons more interactive and gives students ownership of their learning. Because many of our teachers use Google Classroom, my students are familiar with the format, as well as the expectations of digital learning.

I encourage all of our teachers to share the classroom code with their students, and I give them co-teaching access so they can add resources. My special education and ESL teachers find this useful because they can see what research skills their students are required to learn. It's a good idea to remove posting and commenting privileges from your students if you have a large classroom. If your district isn't part of the G Suite for Education program, consider other learning management systems such as Edmodo, Schoology, Moodle, Blackboard, and Haiku Learning.

Our students also access our library's subscription services, databases, audiobooks, videos, and ebooks through the free award-winning MackinVIA digital content management system. Our students have increased usage because they can view, utilize, and manage all of our digital resources with just one login.

Hilda's Story

"Procedures are important because they give you structure. When you have a plan, you are more likely to be prepared for anything, or at least able to foresee potential obstacles," says Hilda Weisburg, author, speaker, and adjunct professor. One day, Hilda mistakenly read *Cecil the Seasick Sea Serpent* to a hearing-impaired class, and *Little Red and Little Yellow* to a special education class. While age-appropriate, these titles weren't the appropriate choices for her classes. You see, sibilant sounds are the hardest range to hear for the hearing-impaired, and most of the students in the second class were colorblind.

Hilda learned a valuable lesson from this situation early in her career and established a simple, necessary procedure: "From that day on, I always asked teachers beforehand about the makeup of their classes, even if it is only a quick discussion in the hallway or by email. That way I know exactly which resources will best suit the needs of all of my students."

Librarians must adjust their programs to their best clients—the students—instead of charging forward with the traditional rules. Doing so will increase the students' ability to learn, as well as their willingness to come back to the library.

SUMMARY

Shaking up your policies, procedures, and protocols is necessary if you want to shed the dusty library past, wipe out negative library perceptions, and move forward with structures that make it easier for you to engage all learners, consider your audience first, use your time efficiently, and keep patrons coming back for more. By welcoming your students, teachers, parents, and administration into your library for activities, or by engaging them with technology and apps, you are creating a vibrant learning hub where all stakeholders will want to be and learn.

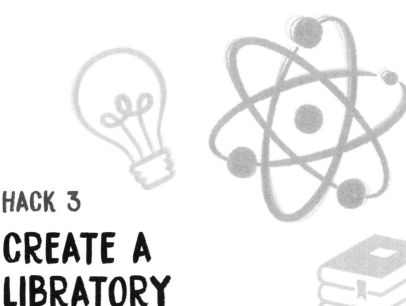

HACK 3
CREATE A LIBRATORY

Provide opportunities for all students to enjoy hands-on learning activities

The best makerspace is between your ears.
— GARY STAGER, AUTHOR AND MAKER

THE PROBLEM: STUDENTS WHO DON'T ENJOY READING DON'T SEE VALUE IN LIBRARIES

ET'S FACE IT: Reading isn't sexy. It captures the imagination and it informs, but for some children (and adults), it is a challenge. Reading for them is a reminder of their inability to decode and comprehend chapters, paragraphs, and even simple words. "Specials" such as the library, art, music, and physical education really are special to students who look forward to this time and place where they can "be themselves"—but are not so special to students who don't see the value. Libraries need to be places where *all* students can explore their interests. This is what will keep them returning to their school libraries, and even encourage them to visit public libraries. If libraries are going to continue to be relevant, we must make sure they have a variety of resources for everyone, not just students who are studying in college.

As librarians, we must create a connection between content and application, and create it for all students. Libraries must not be collections or archives, but dynamic places where people can interact, communicate, and cooperate. Every child has a right to experience opportunities to build up his or her strengths and develop skills to manage weaknesses. Create a culture of making to support all your students in meeting their learning standards and becoming lifelong learners.

THE HACK: CREATE A LIBRATORY

Unless you teach under a rock, you have, by now, heard about makerspaces. You've probably read many blogs and books, followed maker educators on social media, and attended webinars and workshops. You have either become energized at the thought of embarking on this journey … or paralyzed with fear that your makerspace won't be good enough. With so many buzzwords about project-based learning, problem-based learning, passion projects, 20-percent time, and genius hour, it's enough to make you dizzy in the stacks. So you may have begun to wonder if this trend is worth your time. After all, you're a school librarian, not a STEM teacher.

WE NEED TO OFFER OUR STUDENTS THE RESOURCES AND TIME TO EXPERIENCE HANDS-ON LEARNING… THE BEST PLACE AND TIME FOR THAT IS IN THE LARGEST CLASSROOM ON CAMPUS: THE LIBRARY.

But making is not a recent phenomenon. Since humans began walking the earth, manipulating resources has been integral to our survival. And when the hunt was over, the time spent crafting weapons and tools became time spent painting on cave walls. A hundred years ago, John Dewey stated that learning should involve practical life skills relevant to our lives, and that schools need "to become the child's habitat, where he learns through directed living, instead of being only a place to learn lessons having an abstract and remote reference to some possible living to be done in the future."

A contemporary of Dewey, Dr. Maria Montessori, believed that students should be given the freedom to build their own knowledge through unstructured play, collaboration, and communication. Some years later, Dr. Jean Piaget stated that "play is the answer to how anything new comes about." As industrialization began to strip children of their childhoods, these visionaries pointed out the need for play to develop children's cognitive and social abilities. This is still true today, and should be an aspect of our teaching process—and the best part is, we don't have to start at the beginning when it comes to figuring out how to do it. The wheel has already been invented, and we have finally learned how to use it.

We have all heard students ask (and have even asked ourselves), "Why do we need to know this?" The next step, however, is for our students to begin asking us how they can learn *more*. They will ask us that when we give them the foundation to do so and make learning about them, rather than about us. We need to offer our students the resources and time to experience hands-on learning, where they can apply what they have learned to solve problems in practical, real-world circumstances. The best place and time for that is in the largest classroom on campus: the library.

Making is universal. It is not bound by culture, political affiliation, religious belief, gender, age, socioeconomic background, language, ability, or environment. The Maker Movement is not a trend, and hands-on learning does not replace literature and information literacy skills. It does, however, add an extra level to learning, and that level is one that students will embrace. By building a culture of making, librarians can create programs that appeal to all youth.

WHAT YOU CAN DO TOMORROW

- **Just do it.** Get yourself into the right mindset. "Making" is a verb. It is a mindset that sparks innovation, problem-solving, creativity, perseverance, and critical thinking. If you're going to promote a culture of making in your school library, though, you're going to have to start by being flexible and open-minded. You're going to have to provide the pieces, and then let the students figure things out for themselves. The thinking process is what helps students to develop a foundation. Access to expensive, high-tech resources is secondary. Provide those resources, and then use your creativity to establish a safe environment where you celebrate first attempts at learning. Without that mindset, a makerspace will become nothing more than a museum of expensive gadgets and gizmos.

  Set out a plan for how to promote low-tech making and encourage your students to think outside the box. Bring in recyclable materials from home, such as cardboard tubes, newspapers, and bottle caps. Use these as examples of resourcefulness, sustainability, and thrift, and ask your students to bring stuff as well, to help create the library makerspace with you. Purchase consumable materials and invest in a few sturdy tools, such as Klever Kutter box cutters, Makedo cardboard building components, ZipSnip cordless cutters, Ryobi battery-operated glue guns, battery chargers and rechargeable batteries, and scissors. Include resources that represent all students, including construction paper, crayons, pipe cleaners, and puppets that reflect diverse skin shades. Nurture the culture of making in your library as an organic environment that you and your students can develop.

- **Showcase student work.** Remember the pride you felt when your father put your A+ test on the refrigerator, or when your mom used the vase you made out of clay in preschool? Some students don't have cheerleaders, so be their pep squad. Share their work in the library by hanging it from the ceiling or in an art gallery. Display items on top of bookcases and tables, with student information and object descriptions written on index cards. Take photos of student work and display them in the hallway outside the library to spark curiosity. If your students have made it, it's worth celebrating—and the celebration itself will encourage them to continue with their making.

- **Offer choices.** Making takes many forms, so offer a variety of options for students to create, using no-tech, low-tech, and high-tech resources. Students need to use both new materials and materials that are familiar. For example, rather than purchasing five copies of the same robot, purchase five different robots. Have your students work in groups to compare the advantages and disadvantages of the robots, while determining their favorites. Design "Maker Menus" of apps and websites that students can choose from for digital making, such as learning how to code, creating movies (including stop-animation and green screen), and exploring virtual and augmented reality. Give them the choices so they become independent makers, and allow them to take those Maker Menus home to continue their learning on their own.

- **Invite the experts.** Don't wait for the annual Career Day to invite an expert into your library. Connect with a craft store, college, business, manufacturing facility, or even hospital to find people who will share their knowledge and experiences with your students. You'll also create relationships with your community while exposing your students to people from different walks of life. Consider developing programs that specialize in practical life skills such as bike repair, cooking, and sewing. Both you and your students can grow from these mentorship opportunities.

- **Collaborate with clubs and classrooms.** When you turn your space into a libratory, you are doing more than just creating a makerspace in your library. You are promoting a culture of making in your school. Whatever level of school you teach (primary, intermediate, or secondary), you already have allies waiting to work with you. Build those relationships so you can work together to share space, resources, and knowledge. Learn about the core curriculum and special area classes in your school, and the hands-on learning that is already taking place. Offer assistance in locating supplementary print and digital materials. Designate a cart of supplies and an area where students can continue working on their in-class projects. Invite your school's robotics team, craft club, gaming club, gardening club, or student council to host their meetings in the library.

Approach your administration about building a maker club that is open to all students, so they can pursue their interests. Respect that making is an inclusive activity and that each format is equally important. Create STEM/literacy mobile makerspaces for teachers to use in their classrooms, and include materials and books that complement the learning topics. For example, a kit may contain a set of K'Nex and a book about bridges, or paper and instructional origami books. You can also create STEM/literacy backpacks that contain similar materials, for your students to use at home with their families. Ask them to record their reflections in a journal or blog, and share them with the class or club the next day.

Image 3.1: "I'm a Maker" signs help students reflect on their learning, and are useful for displays and social media.

Image 3.2: Maker Menus offer students opportunities
to choose a medium and format.

A BLUEPRINT FOR FULL IMPLEMENTATION

Step 1: Plan, but don't overplan.

After you have jumped in and introduced making activities in your library, take the time to reflect and readjust. Create a mission statement with your students to help give your makerspace a direction, but realize that the mission may change depending on student interests, time, and access to new resources and technologies. Planning a makerspace is not like following the same recipe for everyone to eat the same cake. You might introduce an activity that has been successful for a colleague, only to find that it isn't appropriate for your students. Flexibility is key.

For example, you might not have room for a Lego wall, but bookcase end caps can serve just as well. Consider not only your library space today, but how it can continue to grow tomorrow. Storage is one of the most important elements, so maximize space and efficiency with a variety of storage options such as boxes of different sizes, hooks, and even kitchen accessories like Lazy Susans and drawer organizers.

As your makerspace develops, establish criteria for future purchases so that you spend your money and time wisely. Make sure you're buying resources that are appropriate for students of various ages and academic abilities, and that students can use in a variety of ways. Buy resources with an eye to providing students with opportunities for growth and challenges. Resources should spark creativity and inspire students to apply their learning in new ways. If you're working within a budget, judge your resources by their cost-per-student use. When incorporating new items into your makerspace, consider staying power, and whether the resource will remain relevant and spark student interest over time. High-tech items require maintenance and operating costs, and might include repair and consumables. If you're purchasing high-tech items, go to a company that offers upkeep, as well as materials and resources for the educators. Most important, remember that your ideas might change mid-year based on student interests and directions, so maintain flexibility in your planning and budget for new ideas and purchases.

Step 2: Promote making with hands, hearts, and heads.

Making is meaningful when there is a purpose, and an easy way to give your students a purpose is to start a community service project. Consider starting a community service project in your school library with a Kids Kindness Kart, a cart with simple directions and supplies that students can use to participate in service-learning projects. This will help them connect with their local and global communities. Start simple. Students can create bookmarks to give away using paint swatches, ribbons, hole punches, markers, and stickers. To commemorate Patriots' Day, Veterans Day, or Memorial Day, have students make cards to thank our servicemen and servicewomen. Use rolls of duct tape to transform pens and pencils into flowers for "just because" gifts. These random acts of kindness help students develop confidence, independence, and empathy for others.

Have students transform old T-shirts into pillows, toys, and "Adopt Me" bandanas for dogs at their local animal shelters. Sending Smiles (sendingsmiles2sis.com) is a nonprofit organization that will send you blank postcards for your students to decorate. Use those postcards to write messages of hope to children battling cancer, sickness, or other conditions. The organization also includes a package to return the completed postcards postage-free. Other activities include painting rocks for The Kindness Rocks Project, writing letters for the Macy's Believe Make-A-Wish letter-writing campaign, creating "welcome home" signs for Habitat for Humanity, making no-sew fleece blankets for Project Linus, 3D printing and assembling prosthetic hands for e-Nable or LimbForge, painting pillowcases for children attending Camp Dreamcatcher, and creating portraits for children through the Memory Project. These are all maker projects that will teach students skills and keep them busy at learning—while also giving back to their communities.

Image 3.3: A Kids Kindness Kart is a simple entry into creating a full "Make a Difference" program.

Step 3: Invite your special education students and English language learners.

Making is a universal language, so create opportunities for your special education students and English language learners to participate with their peers. For example, use the Bloxels video game design program and the Turing Tumble analog coding machine to incorporate occupational therapy with computational thinking. Provide color-coded materials such as K'Nex and Snap Circuits so all students can learn about science without the obstacles of language. Make sure your labels have both text and images, to help students develop reading skills. For some differently abled students, a makerspace may be the outlet they need to feel like part of a team. Makerspaces also promote social learning, as students need to develop communication skills and the ability to work with others to use them. By transforming your library into a libratory, you take the space from a dusty place full of books to a place where students are having fun and succeeding.

A RUSTING TYPEWRITER, A CASSETTE PLAYER, AND A VINTAGE CAMERA TRANSFORM A LESSON ABOUT TECHNOLOGICAL INVENTIONS INTO A TEACHABLE MOMENT WHEN YOU PRESENT THEM IN A PLEASE TOUCH MUSEUM.

Step 4: Create a Please Touch Museum.

Access to authentic documents and artifacts can transform lessons into rich, engaging learning experiences for students of all ages. Present history, science, art, music, and other subjects through immediate contact with objects that they can touch so that students develop emotional connections to learning. Facts and figures become tangible when we understand the human stories in our history. Who could forget show-and-tell day in kindergarten? That simple exercise supports storytelling, presentation, listening, and questioning techniques. Take advantage of the growing interest in manufacturing by hosting "autopsies" and "dissections" of appliances, to give new life to old objects. Allow students to take unwanted appliances apart so they can learn about the mechanisms that make them work. Visit garage and estate sales, browse through Craigslist ads, and walk the aisles of Goodwill and other thrift stores to find VCRs, sewing machines, film projectors, and toys for these experiments. A display of these items will be sure to attract your curious students. A rusting typewriter, a cassette player, and a vintage camera transform a lesson about technological inventions into a teachable moment. We already have enough places where artifacts are kept pristine under glass. Presenting them in a Please Touch Museum changes the conversation, and gives your students a chance to learn in a whole different way.

Step 5: Promote design thinking and inquiry.

Provide structure to your makerspace activities by considering the design thinking process. Design thinking combines elements of the research process and the scientific method, as your students explore ways to solve problems with the user in mind. This is a marriage between form and function. Propose design thinking activities, lessons, and units to help your students develop information literacy skills as they research problems, evaluate past solutions, and come up with their own ideas. Work with your science teachers to create design thinking projects that complement the traditional science fair projects. Useful resources for design thinking are DesignThinkingforEducators.com, Ideou.com, and Extraordinaires.com.

Image 3.4: Work with your teachers to create design thinking projects
in the library that will complement classroom learning.

Step 6: Organize a school-wide event.

You can organize a variety of events to promote a making culture in your school. Planting a garden or creating a mural can help to beautify your school while also giving students and teachers the opportunity to work together toward a common goal. Promote sustainability and protection of the environment by hosting a recyclethon, where students can collect cardboard boxes, toilet paper and paper towel tubes, and milk containers to compete in the annual Global Cardboard Challenge or the Made By Milk contest. The Global Cardboard Challenge takes place each October and is inspired by Caine Monroy, who created an arcade in his father's garage using cardboard and recyclables. It is a friendly worldwide competition sponsored by Imagination.org, without prizes, and will give your students a way to get involved with each other and the international community.

Your school custodians will notice that they are throwing out a lot less trash if students are saving their milk and juice cartons for the

Made By Milk carton construction contest. Each fall, your school can compete for a $5,000 grand prize, $1,000 elementary or secondary prize, or a $2,500 People's Choice Award. If you would prefer to do a fundraiser, help your school host a "Trash to Fashion" show, where students create clothes and accessories from items such as newspapers, snack bags, and candy wrappers. With duct tape and imagination, one of your high school seniors just might win $10,000 for college through the Stuck at Prom Scholarship Contest sponsored by Duck Brand. For only the cost of shipping, your school can participate in the "You Can Do the Rubik's Cube" lending program. Register to borrow an educational set (twelve, twenty-four, or thirty-six cubes, with guides and a learn-to-solve curriculum) or a mosaic set (up to six hundred cubes and guides) for six weeks.

OVERCOMING PUSHBACK

Creating a makerspace in the library challenges the perception of a "traditional" library, and we've already talked about how change can be difficult and uncomfortable for people. Overcome this negativity by pointing out that making is one of the *many* purposes of the library. Administrators, faculty, and most important, your students, need to know that the library has not been replaced, but rather enhanced.

We offer other opportunities for students to participate in hands-on learning during the school day, so why does the library program need to be involved, too? The library is a place where students can continue their studies and learn together in a less restrictive environment. They can work at their own pace to complete school projects, as well as explore their unique interests. In the library, students have access to more resources than they do in their classrooms, as well as a librarian who can help guide them and facilitate their learning. It is important for students to be able to apply that research process to their making.

We don't have time for anything that is not related to the curriculum. Explain how the critical-thinking and problem-solving skills that your students develop will help them analyze and apply information. We are all on the same team and are all committed to helping our students grow as independent thinkers. Working together, librarians and classroom teachers can offer students rich and dynamic learning activities. Demonstrate how you can support the curriculum by curating print and digital resources that integrate STEM and standards. Share resources about the importance of play for socio-emotional growth through the National Institute for Play.

I don't want to spend so much time creating a makerspace if it is only a trend. "Makerspace" might be a recent buzzword, but the pedagogy behind it is timeless. We need to prepare our students for tomorrow, today. Our society is changing rapidly, and we don't know what technological advance will happen next. We need to make sure that our students are prepared for the real world—and that we have the flexibility to keep changing as technology advances. Take the time to purchase materials and resources that enhance your lessons and matter to students. Don't rush out to add the newest gizmo to your shopping list. Listen to what your students are saying. Observe which materials they use most, and how they use them. You will be able to create a makerspace that is both fun and functional.

THE HACK IN ACTION

Tonya's Story

"Becoming an Imagination Chapter leader really changed my whole philosophy of teaching," says media coordinator Tonya Fletcher. More than one hundred Imagination Chapters exist in nearly two dozen countries, and their common goal is to foster imagination and entrepreneurism in children. Tonya has used her position with the organization to lead Franklin Elementary School (Mount Airy, North Carolina) in hands-on activities that foster learning through creative play. "I immediately had access to this amazing network of educators and specialists from around the world."

From fine-tuning their Mystery Skype skills with Steve Auslander's students to virtually meeting the head of NASA and other scientists via Steve Sherman of South Africa, Tonya's students have benefitted from the connections she's made with the Imagination Chapter leaders. "Our chapter involves more than five hundred Franklin Elementary School students. We are a group of makers, tinkers, engineers, designers, artists, scientists, inventors, coders, readers, and Minecraft players. We have a club of fifth-graders that meets during school on Fridays, but all of the students benefit from these maker activities."

Imagination Chapters participate in weekly activities such as coding robots and building Rube Goldberg machines. Annual events like the International Inventor's Challenge and the Global Cardboard Challenge offer more chances for children to connect with groups in other countries. Two of Tonya's students won Honorable Mention in the Inventor's Challenge in 2016, and after the school's first Cardboard Challenge, parents and grandparents sent her pictures of students continuing to build cardboard arcade games at home.

"Creativity, innovation, collaboration, problem-solving, persistence, design thinking, global connections… who knew cardboard could make such a difference in our children's lives?" says Tonya.

Heather's Story

"The creation of our school library makerspace was the rebranding our traditional library desperately needed," says Heather Lister, former teacher-librarian at Hershey Middle School in Pennsylvania. Despite being a modern and inviting space, it was still largely regarded as a place to check out books and use the computers. Nearly every visitor to the library was deemed a "regular" and, despite having good circulation statistics, the library was only reaching a small portion of the student body. "I was in search of a way to make the library irresistible. I just wanted to get my students to visit our space so I could show them everything else we could offer. Our makerspace was the bridge to so many other opportunities," says Heather.

The makerspace at Hershey Middle School began with almost completely low-tech resources. This was partly because it was built organically. "What started as a seventh-grader's platform for his class president campaign turned into the beginnings of our library makerspace," Heather shares jokingly. "You see, this student said that if he was elected that he would build a Lego wall. I couldn't let him down!" Since the idea of school makerspace was new to Heather's students and staff, they planned a Skype call with Colleen Graves, teacher-librarian in Leander Independent School District in Texas. Heather's students were able to ask questions of other student makers and learn about their favorite projects and tools from those who had already built a makerspace. "There was such an exciting buzz about the library. Students were going home telling their parents, and because of it, the community was ready and eager to support us in any capacity," says Heather.

What started as one student's idea became a school-wide effort to create a makerspace, proving that even building the makerspace can be a process of community making.

SUMMARY

Establishing a makerspace program in your library is a wonderful way to build relationships with students and teachers who have viewed libraries only as places for books and reading. You will discover that makerspaces will "hook" new patrons and that those patrons will soon discover the other resources that the library has to offer. In this new light, you might also be considered to participate in STEM committees where you can support literacy and research connections. Makerspaces may evolve over time, but are here to stay when it comes to teaching students and allowing them to learn in the most natural way possible.

HACK 4
EMPOWER STUDENT LEADERS IN THE LIBRARY
Create an environment and experiences to empower your students

Leadership and learning are indispensable to each other.

— JOHN F. KENNEDY, FORMER PRESIDENT

THE PROBLEM: STUDENTS ARE PASSIVE CONSUMERS RATHER THAN PRODUCTIVE AND EMPOWERED CITIZENS

TOO OFTEN, STUDENTS are required to "sit and get" in the classroom. However, each young person is full of strengths and weaknesses and has an endless potential for growth. Teacher-librarians encounter students each day who have the ability to lead but are rarely given the chance. As librarians, we should empower students to use those strengths in leadership roles whenever possible, instead of sitting back in passive roles. The library is the perfect place to show the entire school learning community what student leaders can accomplish.

THE HACK: EMPOWER STUDENT
LEADERS IN THE LIBRARY

We can provide many opportunities to empower student leadership in the school library, and when we do, the program can blossom through student vision. Just ask them! Learners almost always have ideas for how to advertise materials and improve programming, and students who are quick learners when it comes to technology can help library users with unfamiliar tools. Allowing students to take on leadership roles will potentially change their lives forever, since it creates skills for their adult lives—and helps to spread the responsibility within the library, which will allow you to focus on other things.

The first step is to get to know the students. This is a task that takes time but pays huge dividends. Spend moments talking with students and listening to their interests, passions, and dreams. Just about everyone likes to talk about themselves, including your most withdrawn students, and you'll be able to quickly identify student strengths. After you get to know a core group of student library visitors, the next step is to locate students to empower. Make them workers, helpers, consultants, and presenters. Learn to step back and let them take charge while you facilitate and teach. The last step is to keep the momentum going. When students become leaders in the library and school, synergy happens—but only if you encourage it.

LOOK FOR STUDENTS WHO SHOW THEIR TALENTS IN AREAS SUCH AS CODING, GAMING, MUSIC PERFORMANCE, AND PUBLIC SPEAKING. ENCOURAGE THEM TO DEMONSTRATE THEIR ABILITIES DURING LUNCH PROGRAMS AND/OR AFTER-SCHOOL PROGRAMS, AND INVITE STUDENTS, TEACHERS, ADMINISTRATORS, AND PARENTS TO ATTEND STUDENT-LED EVENTS.

Once you've picked out the leaders, teach them and allow them to grow. Teach volunteers how to organize and reshelve books, and how to restart, update, and maintain computers or other devices. Ask them to assist other students in the library makerspace. It is common for some students to become proficient with 3D printers, virtual reality, and various pieces of computer software. Why not allow these learners to shine by giving them leadership positions in the library? If students complain about having old technology or makerspace tools, redirect them by asking them to write a proposal asking administrators to purchase new materials for the library. This process will teach the students to research the problem and provide an adequate solution. Imagine what might happen if your students succeed in getting new technology added to the library as a result of their proposals!

You might also create opportunities to invite students to be presenters in the library. Look for students who show their talents in areas such as coding, gaming, music performance, and public speaking. Encourage them to demonstrate their abilities during lunch programs and/or after-school programs, and invite students, teachers, administrators, and parents to attend student-led events. Programming that shares student voice in a variety of ways will help change the perspective of the library, and will make others perceive the library as the empowering hub of the school.

WHAT YOU CAN DO TOMORROW

- **Create and advertise a student wish list.** Let your students contribute to the library's wish list to get them involved and committed to your space. You'll be shocked at how many students are willing to help pick out titles for the collection. While librarians cannot always purchase what students request, giving them a voice and letting them know that their selections are important to you is a big step. Another empowering action is to let them see you creating a purchase order with their requests on the form. Students will feel valued and important when you take them seriously and allow them to help build the library. Be sure to tell them you have ordered their request, and that it should be at the library soon. When teacher-librarians provide excellent customer service, students will spread the word. Where else in a school can students get their requests filled in this way?

- **Plan a shelf or bookcase buddies program.** Certain student library users will always want to help around the library. Shelving books is one of the easiest jobs a student can start with, and you can expand that job by putting different students in charge of different shelves. Have them reshelve and make sure that certain shelf sections stay in order. Students always enjoy having ownership in the library, and this gives them a purpose and a skill that might be marketable later. Many former student workers have gone on to find entry-level jobs at the county library as employees who get paid to reshelve books and work in the facility.

- **Create student worker recognition signs.** If students work in the library as bookcase buddies or makerspace helpers, they might like recognition. Take photos of these students and create signs that indicate how they make a difference in the library. Labels such as "I Reshelve," "I Help," and "I Made a Difference," accompanied by action shots of the students, are a great way to promote student leadership activities. Other students and teachers will see the images and may ask questions that could lead to additional student involvement. Be sure that administrators and other stakeholders know how you are involving students. Their perspectives of the library will change when they see that evidence of student leadership.

- **Allow students to share through library social media.** We started an Instagram account for students to use on one of our library iPads. If students wanted to create a post about a library occurrence, they could use the iPad, take a photo, and post it. We have the students show us their post before it is published, but even so, this allows them to take the lead with our social media promotions on Instagram. It is also an opportunity for us to share digital citizenship concepts with our learners. Few educators within the school building are modeling how to use social media, but the library is the ideal place to help students better understand how various social media formats can be used to their advantage. Help them tell library and school stories through the social networks as you teach them best practices.

Image 4.1: Flipgrid is a student-friendly video discussion platform.

- **Create digital badges and brag tags.** Students love to be recognized when they are in leadership positions, and it is easy to make badges and other wearables for library student workers. When students and teachers see such items, they will recognize those who have leadership positions. In addition, other students will ask if they can work in the library, too. Try to get these students recognized on school social media and local news outlets to let your community know how you appreciate student helpers. Check out Badgelist.com, Openbadges.me, Credly.com, ForAllRubrics.com, OpenBadges.org, and Badgr.com for resources and information pertaining to badging. You can also find badge templates in the toolkit section of the book *Hacking Digital Learning Strategies* by Shelly Sanchez Terrell. Your local athletic booster club may also have resources for the creation of badges.

A BLUEPRINT FOR FULL IMPLEMENTATION

Step 1: Implement micro-credentials.

Plan to establish a system of micro-credentials in your library. If you teach classes, offer badges and certificates to your learners. Tell students that they need to complete a series of tasks or demonstrate specific proficiencies to earn a badge. These tasks might include using makerspace tools, research methods, and even library procedures. One easy place to get certificates to start this program is on the Hour of Code website. When students complete an hour of code training, you can generate a certificate and print it for display. You can also find templates online to create your own custom award documents.

Step 2: Create student techspert teams, library assistants, or coaches.

Sometimes a school librarian is the only staff member in the library, but you can help yourself by asking for student volunteers to back you up. Many students are willing to work the circulation desk and reshelve books, and seeing their friends working will lead to additional students asking if they can work in the library, too. Eventually, you might find students to work in the library computer area and offer technical assistance. Ask students who enjoy working in the makerspace area to teach others about the various creation tools. Students learn to handle responsibility and build customer service skills by volunteering, and as younger student volunteers move up through high school, they may be able to gain employment at a local city library or bookstore. If you have had former student library workers utilizing their skills, invite them to return to school to speak to current students as a recruiting tool and to generate more interest.

Image 4.2: Empower students by inviting them to be part of the library team.

Step 3: Empower student tutors and presenters.

Many students who hang out in the library have wonderful skills, including knowledge about specific software, coding, and even robotics. When they tell you about those interests, be sure to ask if they would like to present a session in the library at lunch or during an after-school meeting. If they are passionate about the content, these students will almost always agree. Such willing student leaders might also serve on a team of library "techsperts" to assist students and teachers with technology questions.

ENCOURAGE STUDENTS TO PRESENT TED TALK– STYLE PRESENTATIONS... A POETRY SLAM... OR TO ORGANIZE AN EDCAMP AND LAUNCH IT IN THE LIBRARY AFTER SCHOOL OR ON A WEEKEND.

If possible, find distant schools to connect with, and allow students to present their knowledge via webcam. Also, seek upperclassmen who have achieved high scores on the ACT and/or SAT exams, and invite them to hold tutoring sessions in the library prior to testing dates. They might be able to earn community volunteer hours or some other credit for their time. In addition, visit with administrators and teachers to offer the library as a space for peer tutoring during lunch or after school. These collaborations add value to the library as a community hub of learning.

Step 4: Hold student-led TED talks, poetry slams, and Edcamps.

Once you've established a group of student leaders, you can move on to more involved library programming. Encourage students to present TED Talk-style presentations during lunch programs, and invite English or oral communication classes to send volunteers to present sessions after their class speech presentations. Offer a poetry slam option for students during lunch, or as a special after-school program. Encourage students to organize an Edcamp and launch it in the library after school or on a weekend. The main idea with each of these possibilities is to give students a safe place to let them lead and learn. Ask teachers to help create these opportunities for students, and even to assist during the programs themselves, for further collaboration.

OVERCOMING PUSHBACK

Empowering students will be transformative to your program and learning community. However, not all adults will be so accommodating to this paradigm shift, and you can expect some negative comments from teachers and administrators. When this occurs, stay positive and push forward to do the right thing for your learners. Remember, change takes time. Be patient and take a look at these potential pushback statements.

What do the students know about teaching and managing a library? They only know what we teach them or empower them to learn. When students help us in the school library, they learn a plethora of marketable skills: customer service, various technologies, organization, booktalking methods, promotional techniques, and so much more. After considering these points, perhaps the question in a response should be: "How can we *not* teach students about teaching and managing a library?"

Won't some students abuse their power? Some students may make bad choices when they are given leadership roles. Sadly, some adults make similar bad decisions after assuming more leadership responsibility. One of our missions as educators is to build better citizens and future leaders. It is far better for learners to make mistakes while in school and during their formative years rather than later, as adults. Those choices can be corrected, and mistakes are always potential lessons learned. Educators can deal with learners who abuse their leadership positions fairly easily, and make those situations teachable moments. Expect mistakes to be made and then guide young future leaders down the right path.

How do we assess student learning? Perhaps we can assess our student leaders using rubrics similar to those of our own professional evaluations. Curate and remix a custom evaluation tool for student leaders, and consider placing that tool in student leaders' portfolios for future evidence. We never know how those evaluations might help a student receive a grant, scholarship, or job later in life. Be willing to write evaluations for their portfolios and/or recommendation letters for their files at the end of the school year.

Students don't want to present in front of their peers. It's true that many students do not like to be in front of peers, but other learners *do* enjoy being center stage. Every student is different, and it is not fair to place this assessment on all learners. Enable those who are willing to present; encourage those who are not. You might also ask reluctant students to present training to teachers instead of their peers, if they seem uncomfortable. Certain students may feel more comfortable talking to teachers rather than being in front of other students. There are always alternate possibilities.

How can students effectively lead professional development or an Edcamp? When we enable student leaders, we cannot leave them on their own. We must set them up for success by facilitating and guiding them. Student leadership without guidance is most likely setting learners up for failure. Each group of student leaders will require different levels of guidance, based on their strengths and weaknesses, so take the time to communicate clear goals and expectations. Require that the students provide a plan and timeline for their activities, and be involved with their progress and give advice where needed. Celebrate their successes after the event, and be sure to always recognize everyone who was involved.

THE HACK IN ACTION

Stony's Story

At one point in our progression toward empowering student leaders, we identified several students' passions for different types of technology. One was a female student in tenth grade who was very interested in robotics. Two other male students in eighth and ninth grade were interested in building with Minecraft. There was also a small group of juniors from our high school EAST (Education Accelerated by Service and Technology) class that was seeking to share about a 3D printing and scanning project. We initially invited the EAST group to do an informative presentation about 3D printing during eighth- and ninth-grade lunch in the library. The young men were a bit nervous when they started their presentation, but became more confident as they saw how interested their audience was in the content. Afterward, they asked if they might present again in the future.

A few weeks later, an education cooperative team of teachers, administrators, and librarians from a distant part of our state was coming to visit our library makerspace. We decided to ask students to present the makerspace items they were most passionate about. This included the team from EAST, the students with an interest in Minecraft, and the female student who worked with robotics. It is true that we could have easily led the tour of the makerspace and its contents ourselves, but why not let the students do it? After all, the library and its programs are for students. Letting them take the lead was the best possible move we could have made because it got them out of their comfort zones and allowed them to have amazing growth. When we asked the students to present, they were excited to accept our invitation.

All of the students shared their presentation plans with us before the team of teachers came to our school. On the day of the sessions, they all did a wonderful job explaining and demonstrating their makerspace tools. The educators who attended were impressed by the presentations, and in the days afterward, several of the students wanted to present again. We found other opportunities for our student presenters, via Skype with other schools, and found that enabling these student presenters was a great way to allow our learners to show off their skills. Every school librarian can do this.

Barbara's Story

The third-, fourth-, and fifth-graders at Jack Jackter Intermediate School in Colchester, Connecticut, are empowered to master skills and earn digital badges. Through her digital badge program, managed through grade-level Google Classrooms, librarian Barbara Johnson offers her students opportunities to implement library skills in real-world situations. Thanks to a variety of choices, Barbara's students have the freedom to decide what they want to learn, as well as address their concerns or problems. They innovate and solve problems through highly engaging tech tools and resources. By the end of each school year, Barbara's students earn digital badges to demonstrate their abilities to express themselves, cite sources, search for information, code, practice safe internet skills, and use makerspace materials.

Through this process, students realize that learning is part of growing, not knowledge that they either have or don't have. Because students are empowered to work at their own pace, they learn perseverance, even when the work becomes difficult, and end up enjoying the process of sharing with others. Student experts who have already earned badges mentor those who are still working toward success, and because their work is digitally archived through Google Classroom, students may also share their badges with their classroom teachers.

This connection between the library and the classroom helps students apply their skills and knowledge in other activities. "My students have a deeper knowledge of content and skill development because of this digital badge system," says Barbara. "They know exactly what they need to earn a badge, although it is their choice how to demonstrate their understanding and mastery." Through this structured program, these students develop independence and ownership of their learning.

SUMMARY

Provide opportunities to empower student leaders within your library. This relatively easy initiative will pay off in both the short- and long-term. It will foster student leadership, confidence, and skills that will benefit your learners for a lifetime. It can also provide you with help for library tasks, and increase student and teacher engagement in your library and its programs. You will be surprised at students' willingness to help out, lead programs, talk in front of others, and teach others—in exchange for the rewards of digital badges, heartfelt appreciation, and the good feelings of doing a good job.

Design Thinking
Problem in a book, find solution
Example - 3 Little Pigs
- Design house + use a blow dryer
to see if you can knock it down

Tie Makerspace to Literature Reading
※Community Service
Make craft + sell or give away
Donations from organiz-ations

HACK 5

BE INNOVATIVE WITH YOUR LIBRARY PROGRAMS

Design library programming that brings curriculum content to life

Unity is strength... When there is teamwork and collaboration, wonderful things can be achieved.
— MATTIE STEPANEK, AUTHOR

THE PROBLEM: LIBRARIES ARE ABOUT ISOLATION, RATHER THAN COLLABORATION

L IBRARIES SHOULD BE staging areas for dynamic, collaborative programs, and yet so many only serve as storage and circulation centers for books within a school learning community. A school library can be so much more for students and teachers, with numerous devices and various technologies that can be used to enhance any curriculum—but only if the librarian is innovative with the programs, rather than staying stuck in the old days. Design innovative programming in your space to bring the curriculum to life and encourage collaboration between teachers and students, and watch your library grow and bloom in response.

THE HACK: BE INNOVATIVE WITH YOUR LIBRARY PROGRAMS

Schools always include teachers who are looking for innovative ways to engage their students. Some are adventurous and open to taking risks, while others are more cautious. Many of the educators who are looking for collaborations are more than willing to partner with teacher-librarians to try new programs, so start looking for ways to team up with them. Build relationships, and let those teachers know you are there to support them in new classroom endeavors. Once teachers trust you, they will be more open to listening to your ideas and taking risks through innovation. Always be willing to find ways to build those relationships with your colleagues. This may be as simple as listening to teachers, greeting them in the building, and smiling often. In addition, remember that students can sense when educators like each other and want to work together. If you can build collaborations with their teachers, the students will start to view you as part of the teaching team—which will lead them to think of the library as an extension of the classroom.

To start with, stop waiting for teachers to ask you about educational technology and possible collaborations. Instead, start telling teachers about cool tools and ideas. Be passionate, as if you are selling the best products available: the library services and your expertise. Don't be pushy, but do act with confidence and enthusiasm about what you share. If you are excited, others will be inspired. Tell teachers that together, you can enhance students' experiences using library resources. Be prepared to follow through by assisting with whatever they may need for the activity they request, and get ready to enhance student learning by thinking out of the box in your collaborations with others.

WHAT YOU CAN DO TOMORROW

- **Host your first books and bagels event.** Invite teachers to the library before, during, or after school to take a sneak peek at new books and technologies. Remember that many educators will accept an invite if they'll get food out of it. Use snacks to draw in potential collaborators, and then show them your latest new tools. Complimentary coffee can also be a major draw. Your building principal might have a coffee fund, and might also allow you to establish a coffee station for teachers in the library workroom. The traffic generated by a coffee maker may spark interest and conversation that can lead to a new collaboration. In casual conversation, educators will often reveal specific lessons and topics they love to teach, and you can use that opportunity to share how you might enhance those lessons using library resources and technologies. If possible, give away swag and books that you have collected at conferences. Plan how you can provide these fun snacks and beverages to draw teachers into the library.

- **Send personal notes to teachers.** Teachers experience many demands by students, parents, and administrators, and it is easy for them to forget about library services and possible collaborations. Plan to make an annual event of leaving a back-to-school treat (a pencil, bookmark, or a piece of chocolate) for each of them, along with a flyer reminding them of the resources in the library. Send personal emails to teachers who you think could use certain library resources and technologies. Make it a part of your process to immediately update teachers while you are attending a conference or professional development session. Why wait to tell teachers about the tools you learn about at conference sessions? Email teachers about specific educational technologies and/or web apps while you are sitting in the sessions. Educators appreciate such individual emails and may follow up and inquire about those technologies and how to use them. This could lead to one-on-one meetings when you return to school, and these moments increase educators' knowledge, which impacts the students.

- **Make new friends.** Find opportunities to attend new teacher orientations and events to promote the library offerings and provide support. This is a great time to introduce yourself and what you do. Ask your principal to invite you to speak to new faculty during summer orientation sessions. New hires are always stressed by the sheer nature of transitioning to another district, school, and job, and the library can be part of the solution. Plan to create opportunities to inform new teachers about your many library resources, and take time to talk about ongoing library collaboration programs. Invite them to work with you in similar capacities. Some new teachers and staff will be drawn to the program as a help base if they see the library in an upbeat and welcoming way. Remember to check in on new staff frequently during the first year. They will appreciate your thoughtfulness as they transition to the new job and environment.

- **Meet with administrators.** Get a feel for what's needed in the learning community by building a survey instrument for teachers and administrators. Find out what teachers need help with regarding educational technology, and include questions that reveal options for curriculum-based collaborations. Find opportunities to talk with administrators. They will appreciate you reaching out to them as part of your assessment, and may ask you to target certain teachers and offer assistance in their weaker areas. This will provide opportunities and insight for you when it comes to engaging in new library collaborations. In addition, this type of action may help your administrators begin to shift their perception of the teacher-librarian position. They will begin to see your job as a leadership role that can also serve as an instructional facilitator. Remember, everyone benefits when collaboration occurs. Teachers and teacher-librarians will grow together. The most important benefit is that students gain new, immersive experiences as a result of working in concert with educators.

ONCE I HEARD A PRESENTER SAY THAT
BEING A TEACHER-LIBRARIAN IS LIKE
BEING A BARTENDER. LENDING AN
EAR CAN BE A POWERFUL WAY TO
HELP TEACHERS RELIEVE STRESS AND
BECOME COMFORTABLE WITH YOU.

- **Visit teachers during their preparation periods and office hours.** If your schedule allows, start visiting teachers during their preparation times. It is no longer effective to wait for teachers to come to see you in the school library, so teacher-librarians must go out of the library to build relationships and create opportunities for collaboration programming. When you visit teachers, ask how things are going and whether they need any help with their classroom technology. Most of the time, this conversation turns into a great visiting session. Teachers are under pressure professionally and personally, and will often open up and share their frustrations and challenges. You might be in a position to offer advice, but consider just being a good listener. Once I heard a presenter say that being a teacher-librarian is like being a bartender. Lending an ear can be a powerful way to help teachers relieve stress and become comfortable with you. It may be one of the most powerful services you can provide on the job because it builds relationships. After teachers get to know you, they will usually tell you about their current lessons and upcoming classroom plans. They will also share thoughts regarding technology and things they would like to be able to do or try. These opportunities leave the door open for teacher-librarians to offer ideas and support for teachers. Not every teacher will be willing to work with someone else, but many will.

A BLUEPRINT FOR FULL IMPLEMENTATION

Step 1: Advertise collaborative projects.

When you have collaborations, always send email notifications and invitations to your faculty and administrators. Some teachers may visit library programming during their preparation periods, and many will get ideas from those visits that may lead to additional collaborations. Administrators will like visiting to see what teachers are doing with you in the library, as this provides a return on their investments of facilities, staff, and resources. It is important to advertise these events on social media and in local news media. Such advertising will also create a buzz in your building, and people will talk about your library activities within your entire learning community. The goal is for all stakeholders to see what the library can do for learners. For example, a French teacher might be inspired by green screen weather reports she saw done by an English language learners class, and go on to create green screen interviews of her students to share with their international pen pals.

Many teachers are unaware of what their colleagues are doing in their classrooms, but librarians can connect teachers and students in ways that they would never have imagined. Advertising collaborative projects offers opportunities for colleagues to join conversations and network with one another.

Step 2: Ask teachers and administrators to make book recommendations.

Another way to build potential interactions with teachers is to invite them to make book recommendations. If you have a newsletter, ask teachers to write about great books they have read or are currently reading. Consider asking them to make short video reviews of a book they love. Teachers do not always have a chance to share their opinions, so providing them with a voice in the library will help build a relationship for the future. Also, consider taking photos of them with their recommended titles. Make a poster to go on the library wall and/ or their classroom doors. Include superintendents and school board members in these campaigns, and if possible, recruit local community leaders that students may recognize. This is a golden promotional opportunity for literacy and the library program.

Image 5.1: Dr. Outlaw, Bay Shore Middle School principal,
advertising one of her favorite books.

Step 3: Invite teachers to hold club meetings in the library.

Librarians should offer the library as a place for club meetings. Teachers who are responsible for big clubs will want a larger space to meet than their classrooms, and the library might be perfect for those meetings. Also, ask administrators to use the library for before-school and after-school faculty meetings or trainings. This will give you the opportunity to visit with teachers you may rarely see. In order to make the library facility a hub of activity, you must find ways to funnel people through the doors and into the space. Get them used to being there, and they will come back. Encourage teachers to make the library the first choice for activities.

Step 4: Host a book club (in person and/or virtually).

Host a teacher book club in the library, or on social media. If you do not have time for a faculty club, invite teachers to join a student book club. Some teachers will not have time to meet in person, but they might engage with a book club discussion online. It would be simple to set up an evening Google Hangout book club discussion periodically for teachers. If that isn't a desirable option, try using Google Classroom or Microsoft Classroom (or whatever digital classroom content delivery system your school uses) as a tool for carrying out text-based book club discussions. You might also use Flipgrid to allow faculty to share video responses to discussion questions at their leisure. There are multiple possibilities for these collaborations, and when you use connective technology for faculty or student book clubs, you are modeling these tools for participating teachers. It may give them the confidence to try similar activities in the classroom.

IT'S PROBABLY NOT EFFECTIVE TO WAIT FOR TEACHERS TO VISIT THE LIBRARY FOR COLLABORATIONS, SO IF WE WANT TO STAY RELEVANT AND GAIN INTERACTIONS, WE MUST BE WILLING TO LEAVE THE CONFINES OF THE LIBRARY AND VISIT CLASSROOMS.

Student book clubs are also great venues for collaboration. If you don't have time to lead it, empower student leaders to come up with discussion questions. They are capable of taking charge during book club meetings if the school librarian serves as a facilitator and participant. Give students a chance to pick possible titles for these clubs, and they will take ownership and plan activities beyond what you expect. This is also another opportunity to invite administrators and/or other stakeholders to participate and see student leaders shine in the library.

Step 5: Visit classrooms for collaborations.

It's probably not effective to wait for teachers to visit the library for collaborations, so if we want to stay relevant and gain interactions, we must be willing to leave the confines of the library and visit classrooms. If teachers cannot devote time to coming to the library for assistance with research databases, offer to go to them and present/collaborate in their classrooms. Many teachers may prefer for the teacher-librarian to be a guest speaker in their classrooms because it means they don't have to take their entire group to the library facility. Be flexible, and remember that teachers and students are the customers, so try to make the offered services fit their needs. If classroom visits aren't an option, consider creating short instructional videos that you can share with teachers. They might be willing to post those videos on their classroom management systems so that students can get the content whenever they need it. Be innovative, be proactive, and keep the library program and your position relevant.

Step 6: Introduce national projects into the curriculum.

Working in the isolated classroom is easy, safe, and often boring for learners. Stop the monotony by helping teachers participate in national events and projects. When we collaborate together, we struggle and succeed together. This is an essential component of team building. The Hour of Code activities, both computer-based and unplugged, are wonderful ways to build bridges with content area teachers. Celebrate Hour of Code during Computer Science Week, Digital Learning Day, or any other time of the year. The activities are free, available all year long, and can be used with a variety of grade levels.

All students can develop computational, critical thinking, and problem-solving skills with Hour of Code. Pair students together using single devices so that they also develop communication and collaboration skills. This process of teamwork will be more enjoyable for students than if they are allowed to work alone. With Hour of Code, you can differentiate instruction for special education students and English language learners. Teachers with whom you have never collaborated will appreciate the opportunity to connect.

Another national project is National History Day. With a variety of presentation options (documentaries, exhibits, papers, performances, and websites), National History Day is a springboard for librarians to collaborate with not only social studies teachers, but also their computer science, drama, and art colleagues. Use National History Day to present to a computer science class about the concept behind the first personal computers of the 1980s, then have art classes share related art they have created. Drama teams could join the collaboration by reenacting early computer commercials in the form of skits. Use the Siemens Competition for math, science, and technology, and give your students the chance to win college scholarships. If you teach younger students, modify these projects so that your learners can experience similar opportunities. In fact, you can even support your school to organize its own local junior versions of these competitions.

Step 7: Reach out to your community.

The power of libraries is in their ability to connect people for common goals. Participate in outreach programs to connect what students are learning in school to their daily lives. Through the StoryCorps public service, for example, students can interview family, friends, and community members and preserve their stories to share with future generations. These primary sources help students develop a more empathetic understanding of our world. The Library of Congress' Veterans History Project explains ways that students can show appreciation for our nation's veterans. Suggestions include visiting Veterans Affairs (VA) hospitals to conduct interviews, inviting a veteran to display and discuss memorabilia at an assembly, or planting a tree in honor of those who have served. Students can support the Honor Flight program by making posters to welcome veterans at the airport. Working with your school district and local civic associations is a wonderful way to develop ties.

Other ways to support connections are through Operation Footlocker and The Wall That Heals. Operation Footlocker, a national program by the National World War II Museum, lends out traveling trunks with about fifteen actual artifacts from World War II for students to explore. The Wall That Heals is a half-size replica of the Vietnam Veterans Memorial in Washington, D.C., that travels to communities all over the United States. Free "Trunks of Hope" are available nationwide from the Florida Holocaust Museum to help teach about the Holocaust, while combatting hate and prejudice. These trunks were designed with tools such as videos, read-aloud selections, CDs, picture books, posters, and other materials to make schools, communities, and the world a better place. The Reason2Smile organization also shares trunks to introduce and enhance students' understanding and appreciation of Kenyan life. These trunks include an introduction about the Jambo Jipya school and its founder, Christine Mwende, along with an assortment of picture books, crafts, jewelry, music and audio resources, and lesson plans. Presenting resources like these allows your students to get hands-on learning, and to connect to the communities and countries around them.

OVERCOMING PUSHBACK

Although collaboration will help everyone, you will encounter responses that are not supportive of such activities. Remember, many people will resist change. It may be hard for someone to imagine the library as a busy place for collaboration activities. Here are things you might hear, and easy responses.

There isn't enough time to collaborate. Educators become overwhelmed with not having enough time in their days, and would rather stay in their classrooms, where they have more control. The key with these teachers is to show them the value of using library resources, and the ways they can improve the learning experience for their students. Every teacher has a lesson they love that could be illuminated and enhanced through a library collaboration. Keep building relationships with such teachers, and work to show them the value of library services. It is entirely possible that you might only have the opportunity to visit their classrooms to talk about the library and its services, but even that is a win. Take small steps and be patient.

My students and I already know about the library resources. Teachers may think they already know about most library resources, but in reality, they could probably be using them more efficiently than they currently are. In addition, do they really know about library makerspace tools? If you have virtual reality, do they know about the endless possibilities that exist in that environment? Do they know about all your databases and digital tools? Stay positive and keep sharing whenever possible, and you will eventually show them something that strikes their interest. They can change their minds, but for that to happen, you must give them a different vision.

Libraries are just for reading and English teachers. The teachers who say this have a dated view of the school library. To give them a new perspective, show them a bigger range of services than they expect. Be specific, and reveal resources that they can easily connect to their curriculum. It is possible that innovative technology and makerspace collaboration options will be good starting points for these sorts of teachers. Show them interactive websites and virtual reality technology if you have access to such tools, and offer to partner with them to give their students an immersive activity by using the library as a staging area. They have a narrow concept of the library, and your job is to open their eyes to the infinite world of possibilities. Help them think out of the box.

THE HACK IN ACTION

Stony's Story

During the fall of 2017, our eighth-grade ELA teachers chose to read the biography *Unbroken* by Laura Hillenbrand. The book is about the life of Louie Zamperini, who was an Olympic athlete and World War II prisoner of war. The two teachers approached us about helping them make the book more relevant to their learners by hosting a collaboration event in the school library. As a culminating activity, we decided to offer a three-day program in the library. We designed the activity to help the students learn more about the 1940s, the Olympics, and World War II through a series of learning events. Since students have a difficult time understanding the setting of the 1940s, we decided we would use the library as a staging area to immerse them in the period. This would include artifacts, videos, music from that time, food mentioned in the book, and activities to help them see what Louie may have experienced. Having a variety of experiences through a rotation of activity stations over the three days would also help students stay on task through the different means of presenting the material. School libraries are typically much larger than most classrooms and contain more technological resources. They can be perfect places to host large-scale events like this to reach multiple classes.

We had to begin planning the program several weeks prior to the actual presentations and decided to have the event close to Veterans Day as a means of teaching students about local military heroes and police officers. The first day consisted of a military-style briefing presented by one of our library assistants. He had served in the Arkansas Army National Guard for many years in military intelligence operations and used this experience to create a "non-classified" presentation to inform students about Louie Zamperini and his life struggles, the sacrifices of veterans through the decades, the American flag, and the current war on terror. We chose to make it more like a military briefing so that students would experience what Louie experienced during his time in the Army Air Corps. At the end of each period, students wrote cards to veterans to thank them for their service. The cards were taken to the local VFW to be handed out to veterans. This was a great chance to provide students with a civic engagement activity as a result of their learning.

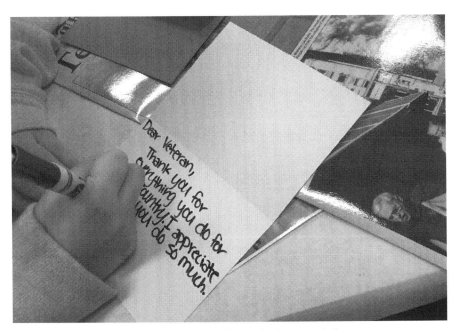

Image 5.2: Students can make and write thank-you cards for veterans
near and far to honor Veterans Day and Memorial Day.

The second day of the program allowed students to experience many different learning stations in the library. One station contained military field gear for them to view and try on, and was designed so that students could get a feel for what people in the military might experience in the field. The second station required students to view a video about the Olympics and Louie's experiences as a competitive runner. A third station had weights in backpacks so students could lift and/or visually see the difference between Louie's body weight before his prisoner of war (POW) experience, and after. Students also viewed photos of World War II POWs and cutaway visuals of the B-17 aircraft. The last part of this learning station provided students with a chance to sit in a life raft to see what cramped conditions Louie and the other servicemen experienced after their plane crashed in the ocean. These experiences helped students relate to Louie's life and hardships as a POW.

The final day of the program started with a Black Hawk helicopter landing, courtesy of the Arkansas Army National Guard. We were able to provide the students with the chance to visit with the flight team and compare the modern helicopter to Louie's aircraft as mentioned in the biography. We also invited our local police department to display their armored SWAT vehicle. Police officers allowed students to try on protective gear and sit in the armored vehicle, and countless students showed gratitude to both the military and police personnel throughout the day. Over the three-day period, they were immersed in the life of a hero through the many learning stations. On the final day, they were able to meet local military and police heroes. The collaboration was priceless.

Image 5.3: Faculty dressed the part for a collaboration based on The Outsiders.

Sewanhaka's Story

"When we promote reading and literacy, we need to think beyond the classics and the print format. We need to consider pop culture and other forms of literacy, such as art and gaming," says Donna Rosenblum, Nassau BOCES School Library Services program supervisor. The Sewanhaka Central High School District is unique in that it is composed of five high schools that are fed from separate elementary school districts in the various communities, each having its own board of education. District librarians Justin Mirsky, Nili Resnick, Joe Nola, and former district librarian Donna Rosenblum agree that "Sewanha-Con," modeled after Comic-Con International, is an opportunity for them to collaborate on a unique project to promote reading. This annual district-wide pop culture convention for seventh- to twelfth-graders includes a cosplay contest, followed by an author presentation. The students then attend a variety of preregistered workshops, such as anime drawing, trivia contests, art sessions, writing workshops, and panel discussions. Workshops have included "From the Page to the Screen," "Are Video Games Art," and "Catwoman to Katniss: Women in Sci-Fi and Fantasy." Donna says, "Connecting with students on a personal level to celebrate the written word is one of the things that librarians do best!"

This is just one more example of collaborations between teachers and librarians that enhanced the learning experience of the students and built relationships on which the school—and library—can continue to build.

SUMMARY

Any major collaboration will take extra work and effort, but the payoffs include increased visibility for the library program, team-building with teachers, and the potential for additional collaborations.

Encourage faculty and staff to dress up appropriately on collaboration days. For example, if your program is about the Dust Bowl, have everyone dress like farmers from the 1930s to help immerse students in the content. Both younger and older students respond well to costumes and acting, and these activities can drastically change the way stakeholders view the school library programs, as well as adding value to the teacher-librarians and their positions.

DIFFERENTIATE INSTRUCTION FOR DIVERSE LEARNERS

Offer a variety of resources and technologies for students

Everyone is a genius. But if you judge a fish by its ability to climb a tree, it will live its whole life believing that it is stupid.

— Unknown

THE PROBLEM: EDUCATORS DO NOT ALWAYS CONSIDER ALL LEARNING STYLES

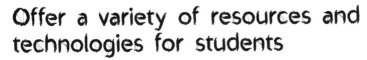OST EVERY EDUCATOR is overworked, stressed, and underpaid. As teacher-librarians, we constantly observe educators and the challenges they experience in the classroom. In a typical high school, they may have a load of at least one hundred and eighty students, and all teachers are required to cover

a state and national curriculum over the entire school year. To complicate things, all of their assigned students learn differently, and teachers may not have the time or energy to address all learning styles. Some students prefer hands-on learning, and others need to sit at the front of the room to stay on task. Certain learners may have numerous learning modifications as required by Individualized Educational Plans (IEPs). It is easy to understand how overwhelmed classroom teachers can become. The library can be an important and useful resource in that regard—but only if the teacher-librarian makes it so.

THE HACK: DIFFERENTIATE INSTRUCTION FOR DIVERSE LEARNERS

The school library contains numerous print and electronic resources that can greatly support instruction. When combined with the expertise of a teacher-librarian, those resources have limitless potential for reaching diverse learners. Take every opportunity to share new print and electronic materials with teachers. In addition, show educators about the latest makerspace and coding-inspired tools. Some educators do not have time to think about innovations, or are too uncomfortable to try something new or that they do not fully understand. The library is an excellent place to experiment together. Teachers may want someone to team up with them for new activities, and that gives the students better chances to learn because there are two teachers and because they get to use more advanced resources. Teachers may be reluctant to team up with school librarians, but those who do will come back for more when they have great experiences.

WHAT YOU CAN DO TOMORROW

- **Advertise audiobooks, books in other languages, and ebooks.** Generate a newsletter to show off new library materials each month, and share it with all teachers rather than just the English department. Other departments may want to take advantage of a resource you're highlighting, so it makes sense to offer it to everyone. In addition, try showing YouTube book trailers on computer screens in the library. Many publishers have movie-quality trailers available on YouTube, and they are interesting to watch—especially if you have that book in the library. Both teachers and students will enjoy seeing your new materials promoted in this way. You can also invite students and teachers to create short video reviews of library books. Display all creations where they are easily visible around the library. Visitors will like seeing familiar faces sharing their voices on the library computer displays. If possible, get advertisements outside of the library walls, too. Place displays in the administration office within the building and inquire about advertisements being shown periodically at lunch, where the entire student body has a chance to see the new materials. Remember to show off your books in other languages, as well, as there may be students at your school who would enjoy reading materials in their native language.

- **Curate assistive apps, software, and materials.** Use a curation tool to make a list of assistive technologies and materials, then work with district- or building-level special education teachers to collect more assistive technology in the library. Two helpful pieces of technology are the Qball by PEEQ Technologies and the C-Pen Reader pen. Qball is a throwable microphone that connects to your speakers through Bluetooth. It will help to amplify your voice during lessons, while also appealing to your kinesthetic learners. You can also make your books and written materials accessible to students with the C-Pen Reader pen. With an easy scan, this device reads print aloud for students. They can use their own earbuds and participate in your lessons without any of their peers realizing they are struggling readers. Reach out to the technology director and staff to request software that will help handicapped students use devices in the library.

    If students are visually impaired, curate resources for them. Find out if there is a library in your state that will loan you braille books. The National Library Service is a free braille and talking book library service for people with low vision, blindness, or a physical disability that prevents them from reading or holding books, and the organization circulates books in braille and audio formats through cooperating libraries. They are delivered postage-free or downloadable. Help students identified by your special education teachers to sign up for a Bookshare membership. Bookshare is a project supported by the U.S. Department of Education, Office of Special Education Programs that offers a free online library for people who cannot read traditional books because of a visual impairment, physical disability, or severe learning disability. The National Federation of the Blind also offers over three hundred online publications.

AS SCHOOLS MOVE AWAY FROM TEXTBOOKS AND INTO DIGITAL ENVIRONMENTS, TEACHER-LIBRARIANS CAN HELP LOCATE AND BUILD CONTENT WITH EDUCATORS TO PERSONALIZE DIVERSE LEARNING EXPERIENCES.

Other resources include the Registry of Interpreters for the Deaf, Inc., and Learning Ally, a national nonprofit that helps students with print disabilities such as dyslexia, blindness, and visual impairment. Microsoft's free, online Immersive Reader program also supports dyslexic readers and English language learners through capabilities like syllabification, a picture dictionary, line focus, and translation. Work with your IT Department to install Chrome extensions and assistive technology apps on mobile devices. You can make your library more inclusive by taking all categories of learners into account.

- **Learn about open educational resources (OER), that are freely and publicly accessible.** Unless educators have attended specific training on OER, they probably know nothing about it. As more schools place devices in the hands of every student, the importance of OER increases. Teachers can and should use OER to curate content specific to the needs of all their students. Some teachers might not have time to experiment with OER, but as teacher-librarians, we can offer to find and curate OER materials for educators. This is a great opportunity to serve the needs of diverse learners, as well as redefining our roles in the building. As schools move away from textbooks and into digital environments, teacher-librarians can help locate and build content with educators to personalize diverse learning experiences. Plan to learn about OER, and start talking about it in your building. Other teachers will want to learn with you.

- **Create a parent advisory committee.** This is a key advocacy tool for the school library. It will also give you a way to show parents the diverse resources that are available to teachers and students. The committee could meet monthly, or at least a few times each year, to update parents about what is happening in the library. Make sure your committee has representatives from each grade level, and invite parents of ESL, special education, and racially diverse learners. Adults will appreciate the opportunity to share their voices and represent their children, and will talk about the library program with other parents. Start a list of a few parents who would be helpful to this committee. Reach out to them and ask if they are willing to serve.

- **Incorporate hands-on learning into lessons.** Many teachers have heard about makerspaces, but may not know how the concept can relate to their curriculum. Some educators have indicated they think makerspaces are just a "playtime" activity, even for high school students. This lack of vision is not totally their fault, and teacher-librarians can help to change their perspective. Use innovative tools to provide students with a voice and a choice about how they present their learning. Seek opportunities to collaborate with teachers in a way that will provide students with time to experiment. If you haven't embraced library makerspaces, coding, or virtual reality (VR), tomorrow is an excellent time to begin exploring simple tools. An example might be to show teachers how a simple code in MIT's web-based Scratch tool can create presentations.

  Open teachers' minds to the possibilities of students building with Legos, 3D printing, or even Minecraft. Teachers may be intimidated by providing these choices to learners but will feel more confident if they are given the opportunity to team up with the teacher-librarian. Show teachers the growing resources of VR through free content on a phone or iPod, or use a Google Cardboard viewer. Students love to be immersed in VR content, and as a teacher-librarian, you can set yourself up as the expert in the building. Make a long-term plan to learn more about these essential tools and share what you learn. It will change your learning community.

Image 6.1: Color-coded resources support learning while
allowing all students to feel included.

A BLUEPRINT FOR FULL IMPLEMENTATION

Step 1: Focus on collection development and resources.

Analyze and update your collection according to what needs exist in the building. Purchase items you know teachers and students will use. Do a needs assessment prior to spending precious budget funds, and talk to the district technology director and building principals about adding innovative technologies to the library. Ask to house a makerspace in the library if you don't already have one, and request VR stations so you can model this technology for educators. Offer to be in charge of VR equipment in order to make it available to the entire building. Teachers and students will be drawn to these sorts of changes in the library, and this will create many opportunities to help teachers differentiate learning for their students.

STUDENTS LOVE DEMONSTRATING NEW TECHNOLOGIES, AND THEY CAN OFTEN DO AN EXCELLENT JOB SHOWING TEACHERS HOW TO CHANGE UP THEIR LESSONS WITH TECH. THE STUDENT VOICE IS POWERFUL AND MAY HELP TO CHANGE TEACHERS' THINKING.

Step 2: Demonstrate video subscription sources such as Discovery Education and SAFARI Montage.

If you have video subscription services, remember to promote them to teachers. It is easy for educators to get distracted by work and forget about resources like that—and what they can do for students. Sending out email reminders is good, but personal visits are better. If you can get to teachers during their prep/office hours, you might be able to do a quick demonstration about how to access these services. This will help to change their thinking about how to differentiate content for their learners. These subscription services yield excellent results compared to basic YouTube searches, and when teachers know the resources are there, they will use them. Share these with new hires before school starts to start them off on the right foot.

Step 3: Provide professional development sessions of best practices for differentiation.

Plan a series of professional development programs for teachers in summer sessions and during the school year. Ask principals to put it on the building-level agendas for professional development, and try offering sessions during lunch every once in a while, as well. You could even invite students to help present to teachers, for greater impact during lunch sessions. Students love demonstrating new technologies, and they can often do an excellent job showing teachers how to change up their lessons with tech. The student voice is powerful, and may help to change teachers' thinking. Ask to team up with administrators, technology staff, instructional facilitators, and ESL/special education staff to present differentiation tactics, as well.

Step 4: Survey students for feedback after a lesson.

Use tools like Google Forms, Microsoft Forms, or SurveyMonkey to collect feedback from students after a lesson or collaboration program. These surveys need only be five to six questions to check for impact on learning. You might also use only four or five multiple-choice questions, combined with one long-answer response, for an effective survey. In the survey, ask students for their opinions on what they'd like to see improved in the program. The results will provide many excellent suggestions. Of course, some students will not take it seriously, but the majority will.

View learning through the lens of the learners. One way to accomplish this is to seek student voice through survey feedback. Hopefully, you can implement the excellent suggestions that students share. If you do, be sure to tell students so they know their voices were heard and valued. In addition, share the survey results with administrators. These feedback activities are probably rare and can serve as a model in the building. Many teachers never think to ask students for their opinions, so doing surveys like this can make the library a leader in accessing student voice.

Step 5: Model ways to differentiate in Google Classroom or other learning management systems.

Show teachers how to create quizzes with varied content in Google Classroom and how to use different types of questioning. Teachers benefit from learning how to add videos and other content to both Google Classroom, Google Forms, Edmodo, Schoology, and the Google Docs they share with their learners. Recently, we taught research for the first time to eighth-grade ELA classes using Chromebooks, and it was a great opportunity to use Google Docs and the Padlet website to engage students while teaching research tasks. It also gave us the opportunity to instruct their teachers. If you provide similar experiences, the classroom teachers will become well-versed in using Google Classroom to deliver differentiated content. Remember to invite administrators when collaborating in these ways, to spread the learning around.

OVERCOMING PUSHBACK

Many teachers become comfortable in their methods of delivering classroom content and may push back when you recommend ways to differentiate, because it may generate more work for them. Be prepared for the following negative comments, and keep pushing forward in a positive way to encourage teachers to adjust for students.

I get overwhelmed when I prepare my lesson content for all learners. The teacher-librarian can be a great partner on this education journey. Provide solutions to the differentiation challenges that teachers are encountering. Some will collaborate with you, and when they do, others in the building will see the outcomes. This will generate additional opportunities for learning collaborations in the library. Do not hesitate to provide potential solutions when you hear teachers talking about how overwhelmed they are.

I do not know what resources are available to help me with differentiation at school. Numerous resources for differentiation are available, and they seem to grow by the moment. It is difficult for all educators to keep up with the new technologies and resources that are being introduced, but the librarian is in the perfect position to keep up. Whenever possible, share the tools you learn about with educators. As we stated earlier, we can't wait for the teachers to come to the library and ask. Show off and talk about new resources in the hallways, in the teachers' lounge, and in classroom visits when the conversation lends itself to such content. Curate resources and share them with teachers to help make their teaching more effective. When they ask for help with a resource, be willing to assist. Make sure to share outcomes with administrators as well, as this is a good reflection on both the teacher and teacher-librarian.

That is the special education or ESL teacher's job, not mine. Creating instruction to reach all student learning styles is the duty of every educator. If we are presenting content and students are not learning it, we must change the experience so they can learn. Some teachers may not accept this, so model it through collaborations and invite other educators to see your results. Also, be willing to share any student feedback with all educators in the building. Student voice may change their minds about their roles in differentiation.

There is no time for me to add other resources to my lessons. I've been doing it this way for years. Invite these teachers to your library collaborations with other educators. It is likely that those experiences will open their minds to the possibilities. Somehow they must understand that there is always time to improve the teaching craft. A lesson is never perfect and should be evaluated every year. Learning should never stay the same—for students *or* teachers. Model a growth mindset by continuing to learn and sharing in the learning community.

THE HACK IN ACTION

Timothy's Story

"Libraries serve multiple roles in schools, even as writing centers," says Dr. Timothy Horan, former English teacher and library media specialist at Hauppauge High School in New York, and author of *Create Your School Library Writing Center: Grades K–6*, and *Create Your School Library Writing Center: Grades 7–12*. Writing centers are important because they offer students opportunities to develop into independent writers, he says. But they're not about "fixing" papers; they're about creating an environment where students can learn to write from a peer tutor, or from the school librarian.

Timothy invented the model for a School Library Writing Center and then created one in his school library. Writing Centers use the library's print, digital, and makerspace resources, and therefore require little (or no) startup costs. Also, students learn to write, and their test scores and academic performances improve. This program is especially useful for special education students who are working toward improving their writing. These are key selling points for administrators.

Students visit the writing center for assistance in everything from developing thesis statements to final editing, and they learn about all phases of the writing process. High-achieving peer tutors teach students about organization, development of ideas, research, and revising. These tutors are carefully selected, and then individually trained to conduct one-on-one writer's conferences. Timothy recruits friendly and skilled eleventh- and twelfth-graders who have been recommended by their former teachers. When students visit the writing center, they bring an assignment, college essay, or creative piece they're working on. Over a few days of multiple sessions, the student-tutor serves as a guide through successive drafts and revisions. However, students may not "drop off" their writing to be edited or critiqued. This is a place for them to enhance their learning, not hand their assignments to someone else.

Sedley's Story

Sedley Abercrombie is the lead library media coordinator for Davidson County Schools in North Carolina. "I have always felt that the library should be the heartbeat of the school, the one area everything passes through," says Sedley. One school in her district has a special place in her heart. It serves about one hundred students who have severe or profound disabilities, and they come from three adjacent school districts. Sedley set out to make this library more accessible for its students with simple, economical techniques. First, she removed the inappropriate and damaged books. Then she purchased more sensory books with textures and sounds through DonorsChoose.org, for visually impaired and autistic students.

Rather than using the traditional Dewey classification, she sorted the books into categories such as colors, alphabet books, dinosaurs, transportation, and weather, and put each category in a separate bin with the book covers facing out. This made it easier and more visually appealing for the students to flip through the books and browse through the covers. All of the books and bins were labeled with both words and pictures, so students could easily identify books of interest. Traditional cataloging was not useful for these special education students, so instead, she encouraged them to borrow books based on their interests. One of her most innovative ideas was to abandon the circulation system and use the honor system instead. Students returned books when they were finished, and student helpers reshelved books using the sticker system to match books to their corresponding bins.

Sedley considered the needs of these special patrons and transformed the library to suit them. "With these few changes, the students and teachers use the space much more often. Books are more widely circulated and no longer collect dust. The simple honor system has proven to be effective. Seeing our students excited to take home their books has been well worth the effort. After all, it's our students who matter most," says Sedley.

SUMMARY

School libraries have many tools that enhance learning for a variety of learning styles. Librarians can assist teachers with differentiated instruction by using a combination of print and electronic tools, and most teachers will welcome assistance and support when it comes to using various learning management systems and technologies. As a librarian, you will find many opportunities to support your learning community through sharing and advertising your resources.

DESIGN CREATIVE SOLUTIONS TO FUND YOUR DREAM LIBRARY

Stretch your budget without breaking the bank

Fundraising is the gentle art of teaching the joy of giving.
— HENRY A. ROSSO, AUTHOR

THE PROBLEM: LIBRARIES MUST BE UP TO DATE, RELEVANT, AND FUTURE READY, IN SPITE OF BUDGET CUTS

LIBRARIES ARE THE hearts of schools, and places where all students must have access to the print and digital resources they need to develop the skills necessary to be lifelong learners. In an ideal world, they would be fully funded to achieve that goal. In reality, though, public school budgets are voted on by community members, and those votes affect libraries and what they're able to do. With the average hardcover fiction book costing about $15 and the average hardcover nonfiction book costing between $25 and $35, it has become more difficult to stock school libraries with books that are relevant, appropriate, current, and reflect the needs and interests of our students. As a matter of statistics, the average age of a library's resources won't be affected by weeding alone. New book purchases have a profound impact.

Competing for funds are also ebooks, databases, magazines, technologies, website subscriptions, makerspace resources, furniture, and office supplies. Librarians are often called upon to become master magicians, balancing their budgets and finding creative solutions to provide what their students and faculty need.

Still, whether you serve a high-needs or a wealthy school district, you can find ways to create or supplement a budget.

THE HACK: DESIGN CREATIVE SOLUTIONS TO FUND YOUR DREAM LIBRARY

Let's face it: The odds of winning the lottery are slim to none. And the competition is fierce for securing grants for large amounts of money for library funding. As librarians, we need to find a more creative way of doing things, and finding low-cost resources can actually help us demonstrate to our students the values of sustainability, thriftiness, and ingenuity. You can also build relationships with your students, families, and community members through fundraising activities. These activities will increase awareness about the needs of your library, while also giving people the opportunity to collaborate with one another for a common goal. Your students will develop a sense of appreciation when they realize the effort behind their success. The trick is finding creative ways to fund that dream library—and it's not as impossible as you might think.

WHAT **YOU** CAN DO TOMORROW

- **Recycle and repurpose.** When you look at objects from a different perspective, you can find ways to use them in your library while also helping the environment. Use cutlery drawer trays and rotating utensil storage to organize office supplies. Transform cereal boxes into magazine holders. Old DVD cases can become portable dry-erase boards, while sponges glued to the caps of dry-erase markers can serve as erasers. See Hack I: Transform the Space, for more ideas. Before you throw something away or say no to a donation, think about how you can recycle and repurpose it.

- **Find freebies.** They say "One man's trash is another man's treasure." Need paint stirrers for students to use as shelf markers? Search Craigslist or Freecycle.org. Want a variety of board games for "screen-free time" fun? Ask your friends, family, and neighbors to think of you when they are doing their spring cleaning. Thinking of introducing your students to Google Cardboard and virtual reality? Post requests for unwanted smartphones on your school district's Facebook page. At the end of a yard or estate sale, you can probably nab that filing cabinet that you need—for free. Search Facebook Marketplace and message sellers to ask if they will donate their items if they aren't able to sell them.

- **Create a birthday book club.** Ask families to donate a book to the library to celebrate their child's birthday. Stick a bookplate in the front cover of the book to recognize the student, and give that student the opportunity to be the guest reader on his or her birthday and read the book to the class. Take a picture of the students with the book and send it home with a thank-you note.

- **Share resources.** Create or utilize an interlibrary loan system between schools in the same district to maximize spending power. If you have been considering a high-priced item that isn't a necessity, such as a 3D printer, button maker, Cricut vinyl cutter, or T-shirt press, purchase it using the funds from multiple schools and create a schedule for using it. Ask your local public library to borrow books and resources for your students to use in your school library.

- **Bargain shop.** If you have access to petty cash or a rainy-day fund, shop offseason for supplies at local discount and craft stores. Ask in person if you can pay with a purchase order from your school district. Join rewards programs and sign up for educator discount cards. Save print and digital coupons, and sign up for advertisements from your most-frequented stores. Ask your faculty and families to collect coupons for you for multiple purchases.

A BLUEPRINT FOR FULL IMPLEMENTATION

To fund larger projects, consider long-term fundraising programs, special events, and grants. Although these programs require more time and effort, they are unique opportunities to work with others. Building relationships through fundraising gives volunteers a vested interest in the student access to resources—and will help you build that dream library.

Step 1: Involve your students.

Entrepreneurship skills help students gain responsibility and prepare for future careers that involve public speaking, accounting, creativity, and marketing. Invite your students to design a product to sell. Popular ideas include buttons, T-shirts, and PopSockets (handles that stick to the back of all types and sizes of mobile devices). During holidays, students might sell "grams" that their classmates can give to each other, such as pencilgrams for Christmas and silk flowers for Valentine's Day. Set up a penny jar book vote each month. Students vote for their choice of new books for the library by putting a penny in the corresponding jar. Use the donations to purchase the winning title for your collection.

Step 2: Plan a stunt.

Students enjoy when their teachers and administrators become involved in fundraising stunts. Who wouldn't love to dunk the principal into a container of freezing water? Ask teachers to shave their beards or cut their hair when the students meet their fundraising goals. Invite the student who has raised the most to become the librarian for a day, or plan a pizza party for an entire class. A positive way to promote reading while raising funds is through a readathon, where sponsors donate prizes to give away based on the number of minutes the children read.

Step 3: Ask the community.

Speak to the members of your school's parent association about ways that you would like to improve the library for their children, whether it be painting the old bookcases or purchasing new ones. You might find a parent with a connection or hidden talent. Reach out to your local civic associations and ask them to sponsor tangible resources such as additions to the book collections or technology. Ask a restaurant or boutique to share the proceeds of one night's earnings. Many are willing to work with you and use it as publicity to attract new customers. Work with your local chamber of commerce to create coupon books for discounts at local small businesses. Selling these coupon books will mean you are both raising money and promoting Small Town, USA, businesses.

Step 4: Connect with companies.

You are more likely to receive donations from local small businesses, but don't overlook corporate donations. Ask your principal for a letter written on school letterhead that you can submit to large box stores in person, or that you can email. Search for the following phrases and keywords on websites: donation requests, sponsorships, product donations, community support, charitable giving, and company donations. Also connect with companies through social media venues, including Facebook, Twitter, and Instagram. Some companies that have been known to donate products are Home Depot, Duck Brand duct tape, Oriental Trading, Costco, Build-A-Bear, Panera Bread, Joann Fabrics, Staples, Stampin' Up, CVS, and K'Nex. Be specific about how the company's donation will impact your students and the library program.

Step 5: Host a book fair.

Scholastic Book Fairs have been a tradition in supplementing library budgets. Book fairs are popular with most elementary and some middle school students and do well when they take place during other events such as Back to School Night and those promoting literacy.

Setup is fairly easy, with rolling crates that house books and products of various cost ranges. If you include the Scholastic Rewards Catalog in your event, guests will be able to purchase not only books but also furniture, technology, makerspace resources, digital subscriptions, and even author Skype sessions. Recently, Follett has entered the arena as an alternative, with a wider range of books that appeal to older middle school and high school students.

IN-SCHOOL FUNDRAISERS CAN HELP TO CONNECT FAMILIES AND SCHOOLS WHILE RAISING MONEY FOR THE LIBRARY. CONSIDER STEM SHOWCASES, PAINT NIGHTS, AND GAME COMPETITIONS.

Another alternative to an in-school book fair is an in-store book fair. Barnes & Noble bookstores and your local bookseller are wonderful venues for events. You'll be able to give guests a wider selection of books, without having to set anything up. The main disadvantage is that students won't be able to shop at their own school during the day, as families must provide transportation. In-store book fairs can become community events with performances by musical and singing groups, arts and crafts, scavenger hunts and trivia games, poetry readings, and author signings. One of the simplest ways to raise funds is through the web-based MackinFunds.com fundraising platform, which helps libraries and classrooms obtain much-needed books, ebooks, online databases, DVDs, and educational software. You can set a specific fundraising goal or focus on your MackinFunds library page. The minimum online donation is $10, and Mackin has promotional materials to send home with students.

Step 6: Plan an event.

In-school fundraisers can help to connect families and schools while raising money for the library. Consider STEM showcases, paint nights, and game competitions. Using recyclables and low-cost materials, build a variety of STEM challenges such as those where families have to build the highest towers or the strongest bridges. Ask your school art teacher to lend his or her talent to lead parents and their children in a painting activity, and encourage family interaction without mobile devices with old-fashioned party and board games. Get a ThinkFundraiser Kit that includes ten family games (cost: $90), and earn 40 percent of the profit from the games your families order. A life-size Candy Land or chess game will make the evening memorable. For older students, consider partnering with an escape room company for a family fun night. To promote computational thinking, host a free Family Code Night and sell snacks and drinks.

Step 7: Crowdsource funds.

If you have a large project in mind, consider crowdsourcing funds through Adopt A Classroom, PledgeCents, Indiegogo, GoFundMe, Kind.Fund, Fundly, or DonorsChoose.org. Before you begin, find out your school district's policies about crowdfunding platforms, and choose the method that best suits your needs. If you have strong connections in your school, local community, and social media, you will probably have more success than you would with writing large grants and competing with many others for funding. Crowdfunding also gives you the opportunity to advocate for your library program in public.

OVERCOMING PUSHBACK

Purchasing library resources is oftentimes a balance between the needs and wishes of the students, the faculty, and the administration. Librarians have to set priorities and make difficult decisions to create a collection that is appropriate for academics and personal interests. The collection must serve an entire school population and can pose numerous challenges for development, considering the increasing expense of books, supplies, and technology. Some libraries have been neglected due to small, or even nonexistent budgets, and you might experience pushback if you try to change that—or encourage other librarians to step outside the box. Below are answers to some of the most common criticisms.

I'm a librarian. I should spend my time teaching, not fund-raising. Writing grants takes time, and writing successful grants takes even more time. That doesn't mean we can get by without the funding, though. Ask your supervisor or principal if you could use professional development time such as a department meeting or a school conference day to research and write a grant. Explain how this grant will improve student learning and accessibility to much-needed resources. Your administration would probably be pleased to hear that you are being proactive and taking the initiative to improve the library. They might even offer to work with you and help write a grant for school-wide reading events and author visits. Also, consider writing a grant as part of a committee. Teachers will be interested in collaborating with you if they see a benefit to their curriculum. Working together, you can write stronger grants citing specific standards and content.

It's not fair that some libraries have more access to resources than others. Of course it's not! All students should have the same access to the resources, teachers, and learning environments they need to prepare them for the future. But each state has its own mandates and funding, and each school district receives a different-sized piece of the budgetary pie. We need to support the students who we work with directly, rather than worry about the students in other schools. We need to be the advocates for *our* students. We need to find ways to make things fair, so all of our students have the same educational opportunities. That means getting creative in how we design our libraries—regardless of how other schools are handling theirs.

My school district should supply me with whatever I need. Managing a school district budget is much more difficult than a single library budget. Employee salaries, benefits, operational costs, and insurance are things that we don't need to consider. We need to realize that there have been discussions about how to allocate funds equitably and appropriately. As librarians, we have the research and writing skills to affect change in our schools, and we need to trust ourselves to find solutions to overcome challenges. Meetings with the district are opportunities for us to discuss the growing needs of our libraries with our school administrators, rather than complaining.

AS A DONORSCHOOSE.ORG PROJECT SCREENER AND TEACHER AMBASSADOR, I CAN SAY THAT THERE ARE MANY WAYS TO FUND YOUR PROJECT. ALWAYS HAVE A PROJECT POSTED. YOU NEVER KNOW WHO WILL BE INSPIRED BY YOUR LIBRARY AND FUND YOUR PROJECT.

THE HACK IN ACTION

Kristina's Story

School librarians have had the most success with DonorsChoose.org, out of all crowdfunding platforms. In fact, I have raised almost $100,000 for our library program through more than a hundred projects. DonorsChoose.org was founded by former Bronx social studies teacher Charles Best. Teachers can create project requests with materials from as little as $100 to $100,000. Once the teacher creates a project request on the site, it goes live to a pre-existing network of education supporters while the teacher shares the project in his or her network. When the project is funded, DonorsChoose.org purchases the materials and ships them to the teacher's classroom.

As a DonorsChoose.org project screener and teacher ambassador, I can say that there are many ways to fund your project. Always have a project posted. You never know who will be inspired by your library and fund your project. Don't use too much education-related jargon. Speak the language that donors will understand. Be specific and describe the impact that their donations will make on your students. You have a limited number of words to tell your story, and an exciting title is one way to encourage potential donors to read your project proposal. For example, *iPads for iLearning* is much more descriptive than *Our Students Need Technology*. For your teacher page, choose an appealing photo that reflects your library program. This will become part of your branding.

Almost 80 percent of projects requesting under $400 (including materials, fees, and an optional 15-percent donation) are funded within a few months, so break up a large project into smaller ones to increase your chances of being funded. To lower your costs, take advantage of matches, promo codes, and partner funding opportunities. Pay attention to details, and be aware that matches may disappear suddenly once funds are exhausted. Use email, Facebook, and Twitter to share your project with friends, family, and community members. Focus on spreading your story rather than just asking for donations. Distribute flyers to parents on Back to School Night and other events, and print business cards with your teacher link to share at conferences. Remember to thank your donors for their generosity, regardless of the amount of their donations. Donors who fund $50 or more may have the option to request five thank-you letters from your students.

Spend time with your students to create those cards, and make sure they're age-appropriate. Your students will learn a valuable lesson about thanking someone. Although not required, write a personal note to the donor, as well. Your thank-you notes are a reflection of you, your students, and your school, and your donors will appreciate your efforts. Express your thanks through social media, tagging donors who supported your project. You must post six photos as a requirement of your thank-you package, and this is your opportunity to show your donors the resources they helped you acquire. If possible, provide photos of your students using the resources. If you do not have permission to show faces, take photos from behind or above. Hands reading books, fingers typing, and feet kicking soccer balls are much more interesting than boxes.

Dawn's Story

"Of all ways to supplement library programs, small grants are best because they take less time, and are often more specified, so don't require you to divulge as much school data as larger grants do," says Dawn Koziarz, librarian at Copiague Middle School in New York, and 2016 Western Suffolk BOCES School Library Media Specialist of the Year.

Dawn suggests that when you're writing for grants, focus on

answering the questions directly, fully, and clearly. The most important things to describe are your students, the need the grant will fulfill, the materials you are requesting, and how this grant will impact your library program. Proper grammar, capitalization, punctuation, and organization are essential because a well-written grant demonstrates your effort and commitment. Dawn also reminds librarians to "Make sure that a grant giver's mission is in line with your school and community." Another important tip is to always follow up if the grant requires feedback. This can build relationships and foster a partnership in funding your future plans.

It is important to conduct research before you accept a gift to your library. "Some municipalities have bylaws as to donated and grant materials," says Dawn, "and you should follow all existing policies for acquiring resources." As a librarian, it is your responsibility to be aware of whether these materials need to be marked or cataloged in a specific way, how they may be used, and the policies about eventually discarding them.

SUMMARY

As a school librarian, it is your job to serve all of your students and faculty. You might find yourself in an affluent school district or one in which most of your students qualify for free or reduced-fee lunches, but all students should have access to the resources they need to become successful. Fundraising may not be in your job description, but it can be a great source of funding to create exciting library programs. Upcycling, creating events, and involving all stakeholders will also help you to create your dream library for the benefit of your students and the entire school community.

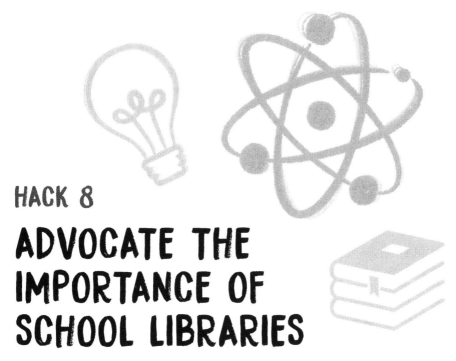

HACK 8
ADVOCATE THE IMPORTANCE OF SCHOOL LIBRARIES
Communicate the relevance

Your relevance starts the very moment
you start solving people's problems.
— Topsy Gift, Gospel Musician

THE PROBLEM: SOME THINK THAT LIBRARIES ARE OUTDATED IN OUR DIGITAL WORLD

IN THIS PROFESSION, we have all heard people say that libraries are going away since the internet provides so much free information. We have also heard that students do not visit the school library anymore. In reality, libraries and librarians have never been more needed in schools. As districts add more devices so that every student has access to educational technology, teachers and learners become overwhelmed, and libraries and teacher-librarians find themselves rapidly becoming part of the solution, as they can provide spaces for students and teachers to visit and collaborate. Most classroom teachers appreciate technology support whenever they can get it, but that doesn't mean that the larger community understands how technologically advanced and important the library is. Teacher-librarians should share library happenings and collaborations on social media, school media outlets, and local newspapers to let the community know. We must be innovative in our jobs and discover ways to increase the relevance of the library program. But it is not sufficient to just be innovative; we also must publicly share outcomes. If we don't share our stories, who will? It is time to change the way people perceive the library.

SHARE INNOVATIVE ACTIVITIES LIKE STUDENTS USING TECHNOLOGY, MAKERSPACE CREATIONS, AND WEBCAM CONNECTIONS TO OTHER PLACES.

THE HACK: ADVOCATE THE IMPORTANCE OF SCHOOL LIBRARIES

Each teacher-librarian has the power to change the perception of the school library by illustrating how the program is relevant in the present. Many teacher-librarians may view this as bragging or feel uncomfortable talking about their activities, but if the information is student-focused or teacher-centered, it will be viewed as positive communication. School administrators and other library stakeholders are busy, and it may be difficult for them to visit library programming regularly. If we want them to know what's going on in the library, we must utilize social media to pass along the events in their library spaces. Use these platforms to provide administrators with photo and video documentation of library happenings, and share everything from monthly library statistics to photos of classroom collaborations to keep your library in the community news. Library stakeholders will appreciate this transparency and look forward to the updates. Share innovative activities like students using technology, makerspace creations, and webcam connections to other places. In addition, send photos to the town newspaper and school social media.

It is imperative that teacher-librarians share their library's stories. No one else will tell these stories for us, and stakeholders may never realize the relevancy of the library program. Post your monthly circulation statistics where visitors can easily view them. You may be surprised at how many students and teachers ask about the library after you establish this practice. In addition, don't be afraid to share challenges. If library circulation statistics are reduced over the course of a few months, share the data—and an action plan to increase stats in the future. When you have a success, even if you think it is small, share it. The more you expose the community to your library's statistics, the more interest they'll show, and the more relevancy you'll have.

WHAT **YOU** CAN DO TOMORROW

- **Display your library degree.** Show students and colleagues that teacher-librarians are professionals with advanced degrees in the discipline. Most librarians have at least a master's degree in library science, and if you post your degree at your desk, it will create conversations about the professional requirements for the career and the course content you experienced. While it may only impact a small number of visitors, one never knows how it may change the perception of our profession. In addition, it may inspire colleagues and students to pursue a career in librarianship.

- **Prepare an elevator speech, infographic, or flyer to share the most important library services.** An elevator speech comes in handy when you least expect it. Take time to organize a short list of reasons the school library is important, and why the role of the teacher-librarian is vital. Your stakeholders may have a dated idea of what the school library is doing or what it should be doing, and may also have varied ideas for the teacher-librarian's role in the school. If you have a brief description of your program's mission in mind, you'll be able to use it when a principal, superintendent, school board member, or parent asks you about what you do. Consider sharing photos and brief stories about recent programs and student work whenever the opportunity presents itself. An elevator speech is great, but when you can provide pictures and videos, it is even more powerful. Telling a story about a specific student's growth in a library program is even more powerful.

  Infographics are another great way to show recent statistics from the school library. Examples include monthly circulation numbers, class reservations, and teacher collaborations. Think of the school library as a multi-service business within the school. In order to communicate services,

share a flyer or brochure to tell users about the services available in the library. Never assume they know what is offered. You never know how this knowledge can improve someone's experience at the school. A specific library service may be exactly what a teacher or student needs.

- **Design business cards, T-shirts, and badges.** Many visitors will take a business card, and this is a place to share your email, school phone number, web page, social media contact information, and blog web address. This small investment may send business your direction in unexpected ways, so take a moment to print a small number of business cards and have them available. You can purchase business card templates wherever Avery Labels are found, and print cards on an inkjet printer or laser printer with excellent results. Consider purchasing library T-shirts and badges for your staff and student workers. Other organizations have these items, and they serve as great advertisements. Countless visitors and people in the learning community will see them while you are around the building or in the community, and that will send a clear message that the library and its many services are important in your school.

- **Ask to speak at faculty meetings and subject-area meetings.** Seek opportunities to share library resources and new technologies at faculty meetings. There is always something relevant to present to teachers, and principals will frequently welcome additional content in their agendas. Take advantage of smaller subject-area meetings to show off resources that teachers can use with their students.

Some of the most powerful connections we can make with teachers occur one-on-one during their planning periods. This can happen anywhere: the teacher's lounge, in the hallway, or even at the copy machine. You'll gain additional collaborations from these meetings, as well as opportunities for classroom visits. You may even arrange to speak during summer departmental meetings, which will give you an opportunity to show teachers new resources as they're preparing for the new year. You may also choose to brief them on new library resources.

- **Document an annual report.** Create and share a library program annual report at the end of each school year to communicate the outcomes of your library programming. Stakeholders invest money in the library, and probably only get small snapshots of various programming. The annual report gives them details on data such as circulations, class reservations, student free flow statistics, new books added, weeded titles, and more, and gives them a better idea of the relevancy of the library.

   Teacher-librarians who are active on Twitter and Facebook groups may also choose to share statistics from those services in the annual report. Both allow the user to record how many times social media posts were viewed, shared, and more, which reveals how much the library and school are being seen beyond the school walls. These priceless promotions are wonderful for the entire learning community. Ask to share the annual report during a school board meeting to reach more stakeholders who may enjoy hearing what is happening with the library program.

A BLUEPRINT FOR FULL IMPLEMENTATION

PARENT-TEACHER ORGANIZATIONS ARE ALWAYS LOOKING FOR SPEAKERS TO TALK ABOUT WHAT TEACHERS AND STUDENTS ARE DOING IN THE SCHOOL.... INVITE STUDENTS TO COME AND TALK ABOUT THE IMPACT OF RECENT PROGRAMS AND COLLABORATIONS ON THEIR LEARNING.... IT COULD DRASTICALLY CHANGE HOW THESE GROUPS VIEW WHAT IS HAPPENING IN THE LIBRARY.

Step 1: Participate in social media and blogging.

It has never been easier to share your library stories with a wide range of audiences. Facebook, Twitter, and Instagram are great places to post photos and brief descriptions of library programs. If your district policy will allow it, use these tools to tell your stories and work toward building a community through your posts. That way, administrators, teachers, students, and parents can view your library happenings even when they can't attend. This allows social media to become a "window" into the library and school building. If you are new to these things, start slowly. Do not feel you have to post on every social media service available. It might be best to begin with the social media you use the most frequently. Create a professional profile separate from your personal accounts if you aren't comfortable sharing your library stories mixed with personal posts.

In addition, start a blog about your library programs. This allows you to share a longer narrative with your stakeholders and connect with other teacher-librarians around your state, country, and world. These connections will provide new opportunities for your learning community. The blog will also provide another way to share library happenings with administrators who may not always have time to visit.

Step 2: Present at PTO and school board meetings to share the highlights of library programs.

Teacher-librarians can change the perception of their programs by presenting to stakeholders of the learning community. Parent-Teacher Organizations are always looking for speakers to talk about what teachers and students are doing in the school. Librarians can present photos and stories about the latest library programs and collaborations, and show the relevance of the library program. School board members and administrators allocate money to the library program, so sharing recent stories gives them an excellent return on their contributions. These meetings are also a great opportunity to share circulation statistics. Invite students to come and talk about the impact of recent programs and collaborations on their learning. This may not seem like a worthwhile way to spend an evening of your personal time, but it could drastically change how these groups view what is happening in the library. It could also lead to greater funding for the school library, which will make a big difference to the students of the learning community.

Step 3: Present at local, state, and national conferences.

If we do not tell our library stories, who will? Teacher-librarians should present at conferences, and particularly conferences that administrators are attending. Sharing our experiences and our students' success stories through the lens of the school library can communicate the relevance of what we do with stakeholders from other schools. When we speak at these events, we also serve as ambassadors of our own school districts. These events are about sharing best practices, talking about students who share their voices, and connecting with other educators to grow our personal learning communities.

Step 4: Create a lending library of things.

One powerful way to change the perception of the school library is to expand lending services beyond books. Plan to add items that students may need, like laptop computers, iPads, Chromebooks, and VR devices. Allow students to borrow them overnight. In addition, think outside the box and add neckties, bowties, cooking pans, telescopes, and musical instruments. These items may be useful to students in a variety of ways and can be obtained through donations from individuals or local businesses.

Step 5: "Genre-fy" the collection.

When teacher-librarians begin to think more like marketing gurus, they realize that the students and teachers are the customers. One of the most important things a librarian can do is to make library materials easy for the users to find and use. Genrefication of the collection is one of the most effective ways to help students find books and other materials within their subjects of interest. It is also a way to help the library increase its relevance. If library users can more quickly find the materials they seek, they will want to use the library more often. Try changing the arrangement in the library to generate a buzz of interest in the building. Clearly label each bookcase or section, and create a map to guide students so they become more independent users.

To begin this process, think about categorizing the fiction collection. Select seven or eight categories that students frequently seek during visits. You might even ask students to help name those categories since this will give them ownership in the project. This will also increase the relevance of the library, as you are seeking their voices.

Invite students to assist you in the process, and allow them to help you devise a system of symbols or colors for the genres. They can help you select or make labels to put on the books, and signage to display on your shelves. Students will be happy to help categorize and physically move the books when the time comes for this task. When the project is complete, be sure to promote the changes all over the building and on social media. After that, watch your circulation statistics increase. Do not miss the opportunity to tell your stakeholders about the changes.

Image 8.1: Interactive displays are powerful ways to advocate for your library program.

OVERCOMING PUSHBACK

In popular media, the stereotypical librarian is usually framed as an older person who is a social outcast, and most of the teachers and parents we serve probably remember the high school library as an unwelcoming place that was not relevant to their needs. This is the reality of thinking that we must all work to change. You may hear negative comments about the library and your role and must be pre-pared for potential pushback when you try to change the way people see the library. Do not be discouraged. Each of these statements is an opportunity to demolish the stereotypes and change the perspectives of what we do.

Students have access to everything they need online. It is true that there is a plethora of information and resources online for teachers and students to use. The problem is that students have little or no experience evaluating the growing number of websites. Many teachers also lack the expertise to present website and information-evaluation processes to learners. Teacher-librarians have the opportunity to offer these services to their colleagues and assist them in teaching about credible sources and how to evaluate fake news and related websites. These are lifelong skills that all learners should develop in each year of their school experience. Teacher-librarians must look for opportunities to advertise these teaching possibilities to their colleagues. Not everyone will take advantage of these offers, but those who do will help their students learn important research skills.

Books are going away. We have been hearing this for years, and it has not happened yet. Printed media is still one of the cheapest and most efficient ways to share information. Most students I visit with prefer print books over electronic books, and colleges expect students to know how to cite electronic and print resources when they write papers or conduct research. Learners must know how to find information in print materials, whether they are visiting brick-and-mortar library facilities or searching the online catalog from afar. They should also know how to locate and navigate electronic books. Teacher-librarians are part of the solution for students who need to find information in these mediums.

Don't librarians just put away books? Many educators and parents still believe that the teacher-librarian merely checks out books and puts them back on the shelf. But the librarian is much more than this. They must be one of the technology leaders in the building, a master collaborator, and a connected educator with a growing personal learning network. Teacher-librarians who regularly tell their stories on social media and in the local news media will change this stereotype. Invite teachers or others who offer this pushback to your library and show them how it is the center of learning and excitement for the school community.

THE HACK IN ACTION

Connetquot's Story

Since 2011, the Connetquot School District (in New York) library media specialists and the PTA have been hosting the Library Literacy Celebration (formerly known as the Library Literacy Luau), a free, district-wide event for almost fifteen hundred students and their families. This event is a wonderful way to bring the community together, while also advocating school library programs. "With the growing number of school library media specialists being excised due to budgetary cuts, and a lack of a state mandate for elementary school librarians, we decided to be proactive," says Debbie Galante, former district mentor. "We needed to squash the mindset that a librarian's main job is checking out books." Debbie, together with the district librarians Laura Barry, Cheryl Carr, Karen Deaner, Kathy Lopergalo, Laura Mansfield, Mairead McInnes, Michelle Miller, Eilene Tarrao-Lange, and Anna Marie Tonger, set out to share the impact of libraries and librarians not only to their administration and colleagues but also to the community.

The annual Library Literacy Celebration spotlights the work done by elementary and middle school students, while engaging the community in literacy-based activities. High school and middle school volunteers enjoy the experience and return each year to help out. Families may also sign up for library cards and learn about programming at the Connetquot Public Library. Over the years, activities have included presentations by local authors and illustrators, storytelling, audience participation activities, designing bookmarks, writing poetry, folding origami, making puppets, playing literacy-based games, and hearing selections performed by the high school's small-ensemble musical groups. In 2018, the event featured two Connetquot alumni authors of *A Speck in the Sea*, as well as Alyssa Gangeri, pastry chef and author of the Mimi Bakes series.

Sue's Story

"Tell your story or someone will tell it for you," says Sue Kowalski, a teacher-librarian at Pine Grove Middle School and a 2016 Library Journal Mover & Shaker. "For the world to know what impact school libraries and librarians are having on kids and communities, we MUST tell the stories." Sue realizes that though we are busy and overwhelmed, our audiences are as well. Advocacy is an art, and "Librarians must be exemplars of getting the word out strategically, and we must influence the type of outreach we do."

To do this, Sue keeps a running list of what she is doing, has done, and what she plans to do. She also makes a conscious effort to incorporate outreach as part of her action plans. Then she shares her news through the appropriate channels, keeping in mind how much information she shares, the format, the timing, and the intended impact. Sue calls this "personalized outreach." Through tools like Canva, Smore, Remind, Google products, LibGuides, and photos and outlets like Twitter, Facebook, Instagram, email, staff mailboxes, Google

Classroom, Google Drive, and the library itself, Sue is constantly pushing out information to raise awareness, seek support, share best practices, and express gratitude.

Nothing should be assumed when it comes to promoting and advocating for library programs. Sue errs on the side of "they don't know" and gets the word out on digital resources, books, contests, events, programs, community opportunities, ideas, collaborative options, facility updates, maker options, and her professional leadership. "Be consistent, be positive, be informative, and be fun!" says Sue. "If your outreach seems stagnant, you aren't likely to stir much excitement. Add some flair, contests, or pizzazz and you will create a buzz!"

Sue adds as much energy to promoting her program as she does to running it. She understands that librarians need buy-in at all levels in order to grow, and she makes students, parents, staff, PTOs, administrators, school boards, and library peers all part of her outreach campaigns. She suggests: "The next time someone asks you 'what's new,' move way beyond 'not much' and be ready to share, brag, invite, educate, and inspire as you tell YOUR story about your amazing program and your role in making it happen! As we say in New York, it's always time to #LeadOutLoud!"

SUMMARY

Many school libraries have suffered budget and personnel cuts in recent years. In order to change stakeholders' perspectives and increase the access to funding, we must begin sharing our library activities. There are many free ways to do this through social media and blogging, email, events, and presentations, and sharing will allow school leaders and parents to see what is happening in the school library. Promoting relevant stories will bring change and support.

HACK 9
ESTABLISH GLOBAL CONNECTIONS
Knock down the walls around the library

Communication—the human connection—
is the key to personal and career success.
— Paul J. Meyer, American Businessman

THE PROBLEM: TEACHERS ARE NOT COMFORTABLE
CONNECTING TO THEIR STUDENTS BEYOND THE CLASSROOM

ANY EDUCATORS ARE not familiar with connective technologies such as Skype and Google Hangouts. If they know about these tools, they may not feel comfortable with the physical setup of the software and hardware in their classrooms. Some are afraid of connecting their students to distant places and not knowing what may happen or how their students may behave. Many teachers also lack an established personal learning network (PLN) of educators around the country and world, which keeps them from connecting with other educators.

The school library is typically a much larger space than standard classrooms and will have adequate seating for multiple classes and plenty of room to disperse students. Most libraries also have a projector, projection screen, computers, and sound equipment. These items are just waiting to be utilized by the learning community. In addition, there are endless possibilities for connections.

Imagine a geography teacher coming to the library to connect his class to a school more than eight hundred miles away for a Mystery Skype or Mystery Hangout webcam game. This activity requires the students to function as a team while they try to determine where the other school is located through questioning. Opportunities abound for virtual tours, guest speakers, author connections, and more. When a teacher-librarian provides these connections in the library, the entire school will hear about it. Engaging in these types of activities is transformative for the library program, for teachers who don't know how to run these programs themselves, and for the whole learning community.

THE HACK: ESTABLISH GLOBAL CONNECTIONS

Teacher-librarians have a wonderful opportunity to serve as the answer to these situations. Classroom teachers work bell-to-bell each period and don't have a lot of time to experiment with social media or webcam connections. They want great things for their students, but they need quick solutions. As teacher-librarians, we can easily share our spaces and expertise to help teachers knock down the walls surrounding the school and connect their classrooms to other classes around the world.

WHAT YOU CAN DO TOMORROW

THE PURPOSE OF MYSTERY SKYPE AND MYSTERY HANGOUTS IS TO CONNECT WITH ANOTHER SCHOOL OR INDIVIDUAL WITHOUT STUDENTS KNOWING THE LOCATION. CHALLENGE THE STUDENTS TO FIGURE OUT WHERE THEIR GUEST IS BY USING YES OR NO QUESTIONS.

- **Participate in online global activities like International Dot Day and World Read Aloud Day.** Find fun activities to connect your students to something outside the classroom by using Skype or Google Hangouts. Examples include International Dot Day and World Read Aloud Day. International Dot Day is all about connecting with new friends via webcam, and World Read Aloud Day celebrates literacy through reading aloud. Participants of the World Read Aloud activity might consider inviting an author for a Skype call in the library. Ask English teachers if they have students who could come to the library to read to younger students via webcam. If you are just starting out, ask teachers of younger students in your school district if your students can read to them. Start by connecting building to building, then progress to finding opportunities to connect further out, and inform teachers of these options.

- **Plan Mystery Skype or Mystery Google Hangout games.** Connection activities are great for geography classes to practice working as teams in the classroom or library. The purpose of Mystery Skype and Mystery Hangouts is to connect with another school or individual without students knowing the location. Challenge the students to figure out where their guest is by using yes or no questions. Check Skype in the Classroom and Google Communities for opportunities to connect with distant schools to play this engaging global guessing activity. Students will love coming to the library for these events, and afterward, you can be sure they will want to know when they can connect again. For younger students, use games like Mystery Number and Mystery Animal. Imagine what parents will think when students go home and tell them that they have connected with someone from across the country or world on a webcam in the library.

- **Plan virtual field trips and guest speakers for classes.** Many museums and national parks offer virtual field trips and guest speakers via webcam, and most of these are free for schools. Check websites for institutions of interest, or the Skype in the Classroom website for opportunities to take your students to new places via webcam. Also be sure to check Google Communities for virtual trips and speakers via Google Hangouts. Twitter and Facebook groups can be excellent tools for finding connection possibilities. These connections are a great way to teach reluctant teachers about using webcams in their classes. The library is a safe place for them to connect, and as a teacher-librarian, your schedule may be more flexible than the teachers you serve. Use that strength to become the great connector in your building. Teachers will appreciate this service, and administrators will assign new value to you and the library program. Tomorrow is a great day to begin investigating the possibilities. Be sure to share what you find with teachers who may be interested in teaming up with you to connect.

- **Connect with teachers to support them as they develop their own relationships.** Most teachers want to try connecting using this technology, but also want someone to be there with them in case there are problems. Teacher-librarians have a great opportunity to create new partnerships by offering teachers such support. Invite teachers to come to the library for their webcam activities, and if they would rather stay in the comfort of their classrooms, offer to visit their rooms to help them with the connective technology. Sometimes, teachers are just waiting for someone to reach out to boost their courage. After partnering with a teacher, be sure to talk about it on social media (if the teacher approves). Share photos as appropriate, and make sure building administrators hear about the adventure. This type of promotion will generate more interest in these activities in your building. Tomorrow, try connecting via webcam to a teacher in your building. A teacher who is willing to try this in her own classroom will probably be ready to connect outside of the school, and might be your first collaboration!

Image 9.1: A Skype session with a scientist.

A BLUEPRINT FOR FULL IMPLEMENTATION

Step 1: Grow your personal learning network (PLN) through social media.

A teacher-librarian's PLN can be an invaluable resource to the school learning community. As I have made connections on Twitter and Facebook, I treat each person I connect with as a potential collaborator for our teachers and students. Look for opportunities to engage in education chats on Twitter, where you can connect with thousands of passionate educators. To find these chats, try a Google search for "Twitter Education Chat Schedule." Find a hashtag that interests you, locate the time they meet, and then monitor that hashtag at the given time to watch how a Twitter chat works.

You can also find many great teacher-librarians in Facebook groups like Future Ready Librarians and School Librarian's Workshop. Ask to join these groups and begin reading the conversations. As you interact and build your PLN, you'll start to develop a community, and while you may never meet some of those people in person, they can still help you improve your educational practices. As a teacher-librarian, try to connect with every type of educator. Since our role serves everyone, we should seek to build a network that will help us in every discipline.

Step 2: Help teachers collaborate on projects with classes in other states and countries.

My PLN connections have provided many possibilities for class collaborations, including reading banned books with other schools in our eighth-grade ELA classes via Skype and Google Hangouts. Invite your social studies or geography classes to give tips on Mystery Skype to younger students in another state. Ask your students who are savvy with makerspace tools to present them to students and adults via webcam. There are always teachers in the building who are willing to try a new collaboration. Encourage and support them when they take a risk outside of their classroom norms. Do not hesitate to pitch ideas to teachers in the building, as you never know what may develop. After a successful program, recognize and congratulate those brave teachers on social media.

Step 3: Encourage student-led classroom presentations via webcam.

We have actively sought opportunities for our students to share everything via webcam, from robotics to reading picture books to young students. Students love to connect using those technologies, and you can create a connection with virtually any content. When you are just starting out, try connecting to other school buildings in your district or schools across town. Also, be sure to invite teachers in the building to student-led programming involving webcam connections, since it could lead to collaborations. Share video clips of these sessions on social media if your school district allows.

Step 4: Invite administrators and other stakeholders to visit connection activities.

When we connect with distant schools or individuals, we try to invite school administrators. Many principals and superintendents may have an antiquated view of the school library, but when they see engaging activities like Mystery Skype or a virtual tour via webcam held in the library, they begin to view the library as a relevant and innovative space. This encourages additional support for the library program. At first, it may be frightening to invite school leaders to attend webcam sessions, and this is normal since you will not have total control of the session. Students can be unpredictable and technology may fail. Do all you can to prepare the students and test the technology thoroughly before the event. Administrators will appreciate that you are stepping out of your comfort zone, embracing a growth mindset, and establishing yourself as a leader in the learning community.

Step 5: Form lasting professional relationships with global educators.

When you discover passionate educators on social media and make connections, keep the conversations going. A PLN is an amazing tool for distant collaborations, whether your connections are across the nation or world. Since 2014, I have kept a core group of teacher-librarians that I connect with on a monthly basis using tools like Twitter, Facebook, and Voxer. This handful of educators has taught me about new technologies, great professional books, and more. They have also been an invaluable team with which I can connect our learning community.

OVERCOMING PUSHBACK

While being a connected educator can have amazing results for both individuals and the entire learning community, few educators are practicing connecting. They have many reasons for this reality, and you will hear excuses from teachers who resist moving forward and connecting with others. Do not worry about those who refuse to try something new. Instead, focus on the educators who want to grow. The following are common negative responses and easy answers.

I don't know how to use technology. This is a teacher-librarian's opportunity to support the teachers by teaching them how to do just that. Schedule times to meet with the teachers to show them how to make connections via webcam, and then show them things like virtual field trips. Assure the teachers you will be there with them for the sessions should something go wrong, and do not be surprised if they want you to take the lead during the session. Give them and their students a great experience, and they will come back for more. In addition, they will tell others in the building, which will likely bring you more connection opportunities.

I don't have the technology or the connections to do this. Many teachers will say they do not have the technology or the connections to collaborate with others outside of the school walls. I wonder how many webcams are sitting in school libraries across the country, just waiting to help inspire children by giving them a larger view of their world. If teachers do not have the technology, provide it in the school library. If they lack the connections, provide *your* network and model how to grow this network so that teachers will begin building their own PLNs.

My students don't know how to act; I'm certainly not going to put them on a webcam. When teachers say this, it is an opportunity for you to team up with them to provide webcam etiquette and instruction to their students. I have yet to see students misbehave on a webcam connection when they are given clear expectations. Take the time to explain to the learners your webcam behavior standards. Model what those desired behaviors should be, and have them practice speaking slowly and clearly. In reality, students probably want to connect more than the teachers do. If you give them an opportunity to prove they can be successful on camera, they will. After they connect, they will want more connection opportunities.

THE HACK IN ACTION

Stony's Story

I recall meeting Àngels Soriano Sanchez, an English teacher in Valencia, Spain, on Twitter sometime during the 2015–2016 school year. I remember talking about Skype with Àngels and learning about Skype Translator from her during our interactions on social media. One day during the summer of 2016, we tried connecting via Skype for the first time. Since my Spanish was rusty, I tested the Skype Translator tool with success while I visited with Àngels. The thought came to mind of connecting our students for a webcam session, because how often do students learn foreign languages, but never get to practice the skills in real life? The only way to improve communication skills in a new language is to use and develop the fundamentals. I began talking to all three of our Spanish teachers at Lakeside High School, and two of the teachers were interested in connecting with Àngels and her students around the Day of the Dead in November. They wanted to share their ofrendas with their new friends in Spain.

We had to plan carefully since there was a seven-hour time difference between our countries, and as a teacher-librarian, I assumed the responsibility of working out the time of the connection with everyone. When we connected our students to talk about their ofrendas, I remember how nervous they were to speak in Spanish with the students in Valencia. The students in the AP Spanish class from our school were in charge of presenting, and they did a wonderful job. The connection over Skype was flawless. The learners and teachers on both sides of the webcams stepped out of their comfort zones that day, and I knew this was a great thing for our learning community.

We decided to have our schools connect again to practice speaking English and Spanish, and Àngels and Mrs. Carmen Christner, our AP Spanish teacher, used Skype to connect and plan a second meeting for their students. Àngels wanted to have her students read informative texts in English for the next session, while Carmen sought to have her learners practice speaking in Spanish again. Both teachers also wanted to have their students visit and share details about their different cultures.

On the day of the connection, each side was able to accomplish these goals. My favorite part was when they talked about extracurricular activities at both schools. All the students were able to talk about their various sports interests, and as an added bonus, the students sang Christmas carols together, since it was close to the holidays. It was a wonderful cultural exchange that I will never forget. Most important, the students will never forget the experience and they left wanting more.

Reflecting back on this journey, a few things come to the surface. First, the teachers didn't have time to seek these connections on their own, but I was able to provide them with an international member of my Twitter PLN. Second, the teachers probably didn't want to attempt a Skype connection on their own, with all the other things they have going on in the classroom, but they could rely on me to take care of the technology and bring their kids to the library for the sessions. The most important point is that we all stepped out of our comfort zones for the Skype calls. There was always a chance that technology would fail, or that the students would not pronounce their new languages correctly, but it all came together for the two sessions, and we all grew from the experience. Imagine how our students felt about the school library as a result of the occurrence! They saw it as an extension of the classroom and a place to connect outside of the school walls. I hope they went home to tell their parents and families about the experience because these are the stories that cause a positive buzz in the community.

THE DAY OF THE CONNECTION, THE STUDENTS ENTERED THE LIBRARY WITH A HUM OF EXCITEMENT AND NERVOUSNESS. WHEN THE GOOGLE HANGOUT BEGAN, THEY TOOK TURNS INTRODUCING THEMSELVES ON CAMERA. THE LEARNERS' FACES LIT UP WHEN THEY HEARD THEIR WISCONSIN PEN PALS SAY THEIR NAMES.

Cindy's Story

My wife, Cindy Evans, is a K–6 teacher-librarian at Hot Springs Intermediate/Park Magnet School in Hot Springs, Arkansas. After seeing the power in connecting beyond the school walls, she began looking for opportunities to use Google Hangouts with her teachers and students. She found out that one of the fifth-grade language arts teachers had his students writing letters to student pen pals in Wisconsin. They were practicing writing and using the U.S. mail to send and receive letters instead of email. Cindy thought this could be an excellent chance to collaborate and connect in the library. She pitched the idea to the teacher about having his students come to the library to meet their distant pen pals face-to-face, using Google Hangouts. The teacher was immediately excited about the possibility and accepted the invitation.

Arrangements were made as Cindy's colleague communicated with the teacher in Wisconsin, and Cindy and the teacher did a test connection with the school in Wisconsin prior to their class activity. The Google Hangout test session was a success, and the teachers worked together on camera to plan what their students would do when they met again for the actual event.

The day of the connection, the students entered the library with a hum of excitement and nervousness. When the Google Hangout began, they took turns introducing themselves on camera. The learners' faces lit up when they heard their Wisconsin pen pals say their names. After this, students from both locations talked about the things they enjoyed doing, and one student even shared her talent for singing. It was a fun time as they compared similarities and differences, even though they were in separate parts of the country. As the connection drew to a close, the teachers made the decision to connect again toward the end of the year, so the students could compare what they had learned in the fifth grade. That second connection took place just as planned, and was a great success. Cindy invited her building principal to be a part of the second collaboration, and the principal even asked if she could talk to the students from Wisconsin. This is an example of how teacher-librarians can meet teachers where they are and help them enhance their activities with technology.

Kimberly's Story

"Buncee is my tool of choice for making global connections because it's super easy for my students to use. It also has great graphics and other tools to make fun presentations by students," says Kimberly Michelle Howell, media specialist at Palm Terrace Elementary School in Daytona Beach, Florida. The Buncee web tool is a favorite with librarians, especially in elementary and middle school, because it includes multiple ways to share student work, making it easy to communicate with classrooms that may not use Buncee.

Kimberly shares, "When I signed up for Buncee Buddies, I was hoping for it to be a quick project between classrooms that use Buncee, but it has morphed into something much bigger!" After participating in a session at EdCamp Tampa Bay with Fran Sircusa (@ProfeEdTech), she was inspired to find Buncee Buddies. Sharing through tweets, Instagram posts, and Facebook cross-posts, Kimberly found herself inundated with requests to partner with classrooms around the world. Since then, she has become involved with classrooms in the International School Award (ISA) Project for Global Education Facebook group. She also serves as a diplomat for Project Education, to help further their quest to educate students about the Sustainable Development Goals, leading the world's young people to design solutions to some of our most pressing problems.

Kimberly believes that it's important to build global connections with students because this is the world they are growing up in. When building global connections, we build an understanding of other people and cultures, making communication and collaboration across the globe more seamless. Kimberly's students are as excited as she is to connect with the world, and even came in before the school day began so they could Skype with a class in Turkey. They are becoming global citizens as they are exchanging culture boxes with a class in Pakistan and cultural dances with a school in Nepal, and are in the planning stages of projects with other classes. "I am attempting to do these projects with as many classes as I can," Kimberly says, "in order to prepare them not for a specific job, but to work with people from other cultures, by building their understanding of the world." Through global connections, we build bridges, not chasms.

SUMMARY

Connecting outside of your school allows students and teachers to access the much larger world. It also provides virtual access to places far away, and to professionals who are not able to physically visit the school. The school library is an ideal place to encourage such connections and collaborations.

HACK 10
CELEBRATE READING EVERY TIME AND EVERYWHERE
Promote a reading culture within the library, school, and community

We read to know we're not alone.

— WILLIAM NICHOLSON, AUTHOR

THE PROBLEM: STUDENTS VIEW THEMSELVES AS READERS OR NONREADERS

ID YOU KNOW that 75 percent of state prison inmates can be classified as low literate (*U.S. Department of Justice, Rand Report: Evaluating the Effectiveness of Correctional Education*)? Words surround us everywhere, every day, and lacking the ability to read them can isolate people from the larger learning community. Being able to read is a skill that many of us take for granted, but it is fundamental for other learning.

With increasing emphasis on high-stakes testing, is it any wonder that many kids have started to view reading as a chore instead of something that might be fun? Their feelings toward reading develop as soon as they are old enough to hold a book, but change over time depending on how they're exposed to books. For shy children, being asked to read aloud in class is traumatizing, and for those who have trouble reading, teacher expectations become frightening. Attitudes about reading continue into adulthood and can affect future academic success, so when we come across students who are resistant to books—or think they're not good readers—we must find a way to help them discover the joy of reading.

THE HACK: CELEBRATE READING EVERY TIME AND EVERYWHERE

I don't believe in nonreaders or reluctant readers; they are yet-to-be readers! I believe in children who haven't *yet* connected with reading. That connection will happen when they discover books that speak to them, regardless of the topic and reading level. It can be a book in a different format, such as an ebook or an audiobook, or it could be sharing the reading experience with another person. Reading doesn't have to be a solitary activity—it can be an event that brings people together—but it should always be enjoyable.

For that to happen, we as librarians need to figure out how to embrace all readers and find ways to make reading enjoyable no matter how skilled those readers are. We need to celebrate reading and encourage our students to read for pleasure as well as for information. We need to provide access to a variety of digital and print resources because we never know what will speak to different readers. We need to purchase a variety of books that students *want* to read. That is how we can promote lifelong learning. To educate our students, we need to celebrate reading in all its forms, rather than expecting all students to adhere to the old-fashioned ideas of what reading is.

WHAT YOU CAN DO TOMORROW

- **Make book circulation exciting.** Rather than shelving those new books as soon as you process them, display them on the tops of your bookcases and at the circulation desk. Who can resist the shiny covers and crisp binding of new books? Invite your colleagues and students to preview them and enter a lottery to be the first to read them. Create "express" book bundles of similar titles, authors, and genres for students to check out. Insert book bubble bookmarks that "speak" to students and feature messages such as "Choose me" and "Take me home." Pique your students' curiosity by covering a variety of books in plain brown or wrapping paper, then writing hints on the paper about what the book inside might hold. Featuring your books in these ways and making them exciting can attract students who might have thought that the library wasn't for them.

CREATE BUTTONS OR PRINT STICKERS FOR STUDENTS, FACULTY, ADMINISTRATORS, GUIDANCE COUNSELORS, PARAPROFESSIONALS, LUNCH LADIES, AND CUSTODIANS TO WEAR THAT SAY, "ASK ME WHAT I'M READING" TO SPARK CONVERSATIONS.

- **Match readers.** Matchmaking is a fine art, and librarians are experts at it. Pay attention to circulation trends so that you can start to match students together to form reading groups. Match older and younger readers to create "reading buddies." Use Flipgrid, Skype, or Google Hangouts to connect your students to reading buddies from all over the world. Create a "Readers Wanted" board, where students can post their favorite authors, books, and genres, and then find new reading friends with similar interests. Set aside books with specific students in mind, and put notes inside explaining how you chose those particular books for them.

- **Extend the library.** Help to promote reading *beyond* the library in order to reach a larger community of readers. Work with your administrators or PTO to create classroom libraries throughout the school, and in places such as cafeterias, guidance departments, and offices. Encourage students to donate books and magazines they no longer read, and place them in Little Free Libraries scattered throughout the building. Create a book cart of eye-catching fiction and nonfiction books, grab a mobile device and a wireless scanner, and visit the cafeteria once a month during your students' lunch periods to circulate. If students don't think the library is for them, they won't visit—which means you have to go out and find them.

- **Share books.** Greet your students with a book in your hand as they enter the library. Create buttons or print stickers for students, faculty, administrators, guidance counselors, paraprofessionals, lunch ladies, and custodians to wear that say, "Ask me what I'm reading" to spark conversations. Use the site WhatImReading.org to create "What I'm Reading" posters to hang on doors, in hallways, and even bathrooms. Ask to add a book title each day to the online and printed lunch menus.

Encourage students to take "shelfie" pictures of themselves with their favorite books, and create BookSnaps of key parts of books to post online or in the school paper. Share book talks over the loudspeaker during morning announcements, and capture the moment with Facebook Live or Twitter Live. Ask the school newspaper advisor to include a book recommendation column. Share pictures on a Padlet so students, parents, and teachers can access them through email, Twitter, Facebook, and Remind. Curate book lists for home mailings, backpacks, and Back to School Night. Package both nonfiction and fiction books into popular topics of interest (If you like Harry Potter, check out these other titles ...). Provide your school administrators, superintendent, and school board members with book recommendations they can mention during meetings, share through the district website, or add to home mailings. The larger your network for book-sharing becomes, the more future readers you'll be able to reach!

- **Include your students.** Libraries have limited budgets, and we can't order every book we want. But part of your budget should be set aside for student requests. Create a reader's advisory, establish a book-selection committee, or distribute a simple book recommendation form. Plan a field trip to the local bookstore so your students can shop for books to add to the collection. Whether you order ten or one hundred of these student-selected books, make sure to advertise them. Create a display of these books, with photos of the students who selected them. Stick a "This book was recommended by _____" label on the cover. Children are more likely to respect their peers' opinions than yours. Set aside a portion of your budget to order multiple copies of titles for student-led book clubs. If possible, download the audiobook or borrow it from the public library. Purchase those graphic novels that your students love so much, but intersperse them throughout the collection to encourage your students to extend their interests. A simple colored label on the spine can indicate that they have discovered a graphic novel.

A BLUEPRINT FOR FULL IMPLEMENTATION

So you have your students hooked on reading, but how do you keep the momentum going? Over the school year, and even during the summer, you can promote a reading culture through programs and events that your students will remember long after they graduate.

Step 1: Document reading.

Just as athletes build stamina through exercise, weightlifting, and training, your students can set reading goals and milestones. Inspire them to create paper or digital journals of what they are reading. Create a punch-card program where students can earn prizes or experiences such as an invitation to a VIP Readers Party with more books read, just like those summer reading programs where students report on the titles that they read out of school. Offer printouts of circulation habits so your students can create their own databases of the books they have read and plan to read in the future. Show them how to create an account through Goodreads, Bookopolis, or Biblionasium to track their reading history and write book recommendations. Integrate these with your book circulation software, if possible. Visit English classes and teach students how to write blogs or create podcasts about books. Two student-friendly tools for this are Kidblog and Weebly for Education.

USE MOBILE DEVICES TO CREATE PROFESSIONAL-LOOKING BOOK TRAILERS AND RECOMMENDATIONS, AND THEN POST THEM ON YOUTUBE OR ARCHIVE AND SHARE THEM THROUGH A GOOGLE LINK. TEACH YOUR STUDENTS AND TEACHERS HOW TO DO THE SAME SO THEY GET INVOLVED, TOO.

Step 2: Create a world of literacy artwork.

Seek the blank canvases in your school that have been ignored, and make them billboards for literacy. Lockers and the front-sides of steps are the perfect rectangular shapes for oversized book spines. Divide the hallways into different Dewey nonfiction sections or fiction genres, and give your students the opportunity to bring those sterile spaces to life. For high school students, parking spaces provide canvases for covers of favorite books. Do you want to inspire visitors to come to your school on rainy days? Use stencils and waterproof spray to apply famous quotes of literature on the sidewalk near your front entrance, then cover them in chalks so that the sayings only show up when the rain rolls across the concrete.

Step 3: Advertise with videos.

Use mobile devices to create professional-looking book trailers and recommendations, and then post them on YouTube or archive and share them through a Google link. Teach your students and teachers how to do the same so they get involved, too. Tools for videoing include Adobe Spark Video, Animoto, iMovie, My Simple Show, Kizoa, Biteable, WeVideo, and TouchCast. For green screen options, consider the Doink Green Screen or TouchCast apps, or the web-based WeVideo. Exercise your vocal cords and create a song parody or a music video about the library and reading. Create a mannequin challenge, not only in the library but around the school, where students take pictures of other students and faculty caught with books.

Step 4: Run a contest.

Running school-wide contests is a wonderful way to promote reading and healthy competition. Create a bookmark-designing contest, then print multiples of the winner and pass them out when students check out books. Create theme contests that change with the seasons, such as designing a book-themed pumpkin, ornament, or flag. Involve your faculty in the fun. Display pictures of them as children holding books, then ask your students to match the baby pictures with the adult pictures.

For school-wide celebrations during book fairs or other library-related holidays, hold a door-decorating contest. This is a wonderful opportunity for students to cooperate and create award-winning designs, and for content-area teachers to share their own love of reading. Remember to advertise the contest and give at least three weeks' notice so teachers can work with their students to decide on a book or theme, gather materials, and design their doors. Take photos of each door and incorporate these images into a Google survey so that the entire student body can vote for their favorites. Use some of your book fair profits and invite the winning students and teachers to shop for their awards. The entire school will begin to look forward to this team-building event each year, and the competition can become fierce. Some classes might even begin designing their doors and collecting materials months in advance.

Image 10.1: Doors decorated with popular books create literacy-rich school hallways.

Image 10.2: Harry Potter welcomed students through the door.

Image 10.3: Students contributed their own self-descriptions to this book-themed door.

Step 5: Promote reading programs.

We all appreciate the value of reading and its effect on other subject areas, but do we ever give our students time to just read for pleasure? Once a month (or week), designate a time for the kids to drop everything and read a book or a magazine. Invite people in person or virtually to share books during World Read Aloud Day. Hold a "book tasting" or "speed dating" in your library, where students can learn about new books they might be interested in borrowing. Invite senior citizens from the local retirement community or assisted living facility to visit your library, so your young students can read to them. Host book clubs on the same nights as parent meetings to increase attendance at both events. Create a Facebook group virtual book club for students and their parents to share their favorite books. Invite your public librarians to speak to your students about the summer reading program initiatives. Write a grant or solicit community support to purchase copies of *Oh, the Places You'll Go* by Dr. Seuss or *We're All Wonders* by R.J. Palacio for all incoming kindergarten students. This is a positive way to welcome children to school, and can also serve as a keepsake when teachers all the way through twelfth grade sign these books.

Step 6: Pay it forward.

Throughout history, people have developed ties that bind them with one another by sharing their stories. Create opportunities for your students and faculty to not only share their favorite books but also to connect with others. Speak to directors of hospitals, nursing homes, retirement centers, and even a local Ronald McDonald House to set up Skype or Google Hangout sessions. Both the readers and those being read to will benefit from the experience of connecting virtually. Host a readathon for your students to raise money for and awareness of social causes. Transform your research unit into an opportunity for your students to write and illustrate their own picture books to share with children around the world. These personalized international gifts can help recipients develop English reading skills.

Step 7: Host an event.

We remember moments in our lives that have special meaning to us. Your students will probably not remember the Dewey Decimal System or what a copyright page is, but they will remember the parade when they dressed up as their favorite book characters. Develop a "One Book, One School" program and use a book to help your students participate in conversations about universal themes such as truth, loyalty, or perseverance. Then design a culminating activity that celebrates this theme. Plan a mock Caldecott or Newbery Awards ceremony based on grade-level popular votes, and share your celebration with the winning authors through social media. Celebrate an annual "book birthday" for an anticipated title with balloons, snacks, and celebrity readings by members of the community.

Celebrate students as writer rock stars. Students can use the Book Creator app to write and record their own books to share around the world through WriteOurWorld.org, and can also write and illustrate their own books, which you can catalog and house in the library in a special section. If your school publishes a literary magazine or newspaper, offer the library as a place for these organizations to celebrate their newest issues. Plan an event like the "Millionaire Bash," an annual tradition for kindergartners at the Britt David Magnet Academy in Columbus, Georgia, which treats students who have read a million words over the school year as celebrities.

OVERCOMING PUSHBACK

Promoting literacy and reading for enjoyment is a mission for all librarians, and it should include all adults, as well. The more adults they see reading, the more our students will try it themselves. Demonstrating good reading habits doesn't take much time—but that doesn't mean all adults will see the immediate value. Be ready for pushback with the following answers.

I'm a (insert teacher title here). What do I know about reading? As a school librarian, you are a champion of reading, a teacher leader, and a collaborator. Provide your colleagues with the resources they need to promote reading in their classrooms. Show your teachers books, websites, and databases that complement their lessons, so students can develop their reading skills and understanding of the content. Order magazines that teachers can borrow for students to read if they finish their tests or classwork early.

We don't have time to read for enjoyment. Collect short pieces and poems that students can read in a brief sitting. Volunteer to read a few pages of a short novel over the school loudspeaker each week so that the entire student body can participate in a collective reading experience. Purchase picture books with few words and big ideas that teachers can read to introduce topics and use as writing prompts. Connect with curriculum to support your struggling readers, special education students, and English language learners.

We don't have enough funding for classroom libraries. Librarians can find many creative ways to help their colleagues collect reading materials for students without having to spend the library book budget. Give teachers a discount during the book fair, if you can manage it. Ask medical offices to donate appropriate old magazines. Stop by your local comic book shop for Free Comic Book Day in May. Reach out to local authors to donate titles. Ask vendors for the books they have left over at the end of conferences. Reach out to parents and community members, and post a book drop event on Facebook. Organize book swaps in the library where students, teachers, and parents can exchange books to build their classroom and home libraries. Be a liaison between your classroom teachers and the public library by distributing and collecting public library card applications for teachers and students. To save money on adding bookcases and shelving, install vinyl gutters beneath Smartboards, whiteboards, and chalkboards.

If your school serves children in need between birth and age eighteen, you can register at FirstBook.org. This nonprofit makes brand new, high-quality books and educational resources affordable to its member network. The free Open eBooks app is also available through this organization and allows for kids to download up to ten ebooks at a time, available for fifty-six days before they must be renewed. Another way for students to have access to books in their community is the BarbershopBooks.org site, which connects African-American boys ages four to eight to reading in male-centered spaces such as barbershops. ReachOutAndRead.org is a nonprofit that incorporates books into pediatric care. There are plenty of ways to find books for your students if you know where to look.

THE HACK IN ACTION

Stacey's Story

Back in her office, Stacey Rattner, librarian at Castleton Elementary School in New York, has a box of birthday plates and napkins, a banner, a tablecloth, and balloons. This is because she is frequently celebrating book birthdays with her elementary school students. Whenever an advance reader's copy of a book lands in her hands, she knows it could be the next book for her to champion. After she reads it and figures out if there is enough lead time, she will decide if she wants to move further with her party planning. Sometimes she decides to honor a special author or illustrator who she and her students have either celebrated virtually in the past, who has visited them, or is just someone they love. Finally, it may be a book that *everyone* is talking about. Stacey makes the executive decision on when they will have a party.

That was the case in January 2018 when Matt de la Pena and Loren Long's new picture book, *Love,* was released. Stacey had not seen the book but had heard so much about it that she wanted to have a party. When she read the book aloud for the first time during the party, she cried. She and her students ate chocolate and love-related snacks (she even included a chocolate fountain!) and had the amazing opportunity to video chat with Matt and Loren. What a party! Stacey and her students enjoyed singing "Happy Birthday" to their book creators.

Stacey makes books available for purchase, too. It always amazes her how many parents purchase books just for the celebration. However, this does pose a challenge for the bookseller. Since Stacey searches for books to be available on the release date, the booksellers have to seek permission from the publisher to sell them to Stacey the day before. Usually, Stacey purchases between ten and thirty books, though sometimes more. Even though event planning wasn't part of her course requirements to become a certified school librarian, Stacey has become a master at celebrating authors and illustrators, and sees it as a way to reach kids she might not have reached otherwise—and teach nonreaders that reading can be fun. She says, "These book birthday parties take extra time, energy, and money, but are so worth it. You can't put a price on a smiling kid with a spanking brand-new book after she just sang 'Happy Book Birthday' to the author and illustrator."

Laura's Story

For Laura Gardner, 2016 School Librarian of the Year finalist and teacher-librarian at Dartmouth Middle School in Massachusetts, reading promotion is her favorite part of her job. Laura promotes reading personally over social media, to whole classes using book buffets and book talks, and to teachers through her school's teacher book club that meets after school. One of the most important things her school does is offer choice: choice in free-reading books (all kids are required to have one all day) and choice in summer reading books. To facilitate that choice, Laura does book buffets with every ELA teacher every trimester, and kids are encouraged to keep a #TBR (to be read) list at all times. A couple of teachers in the school keep a "Gardner's Garden" outside their classrooms, where they post pictures of the books that they booktalk each week in their classrooms. Laura's school also celebrates reading on a regular basis, and the Reading Wall of Fame is prominently posted outside the library on a large bulletin board. Students can be nominated for any reason related to reading, and their photos are posted with their favorite books. Therefore, the Reading Wall of Fame also serves as another mode of recommending books.

Book clubs are another important part of her school's culture of reading. Laura hosts lunch bunch book clubs for each grade, which meet once or twice a week. Her students participated in the Global Read Aloud (*The Wild Robot* in sixth grade and *A Monster Calls* for seventh and eighth grades). They have also Skyped with authors and chatted about books they love. The teachers at Laura's school also meet once a month throughout the year for a book club to discuss middle grade and YA books they have read and recommend. Laura explains, "One meeting was about books with diverse characters. Everyone read at least one book that fit our theme, and we shared our thoughts over cookies and tea." A leader in promoting literature in her school, Laura organized a Facebook group of ten teachers who joined her in #30booksummer, the goal being that each teacher would read thirty middle-grade-appropriate books during the summer. In the group, Laura and her colleagues shared their thoughts. They met together to switch out their books, and enjoyed a potluck lunch where they chatted about their books.

Laura's social media accounts (@LibrarianMsG on Instagram, Goodreads, and Twitter) are filled with book recommendations. In the summer of 2017, she set a goal of reading a #bookaday all summer long, with carefully curated lists of books from which to choose. Laura met her goal and also reviewed all the books she loved on social media with a well-lit photo, a rating, a summary, reviews, and hashtags. Some of Laura's students even follow her on Instagram. Laura says, "I like nothing better than a kid coming in the library to ask for a book I recommended over social media. I also print out the covers of all the middle-grade books I have read and hang them on my door, and they have already spilled over to the wall for this school year."

SUMMARY

The heart of libraries is and always will be reading. Connecting students to the right books has the power to change their lives. Whether it is print or digital, visual or audio, everyone loves a good story. We read and listen to them over and over and know them as well as our closest friends. As librarians, it's our job to show all of our students how to love reading, so that they become active and well-educated citizens in our communities.

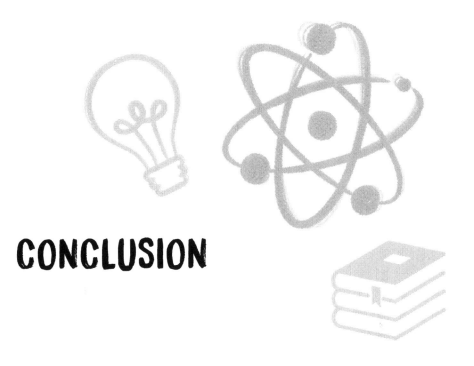

CONCLUSION

*H*ACKING *SCHOOL LIBRARIES* is designed to help teacher-librarians get out of their comfort zones and reach their learning communities in more innovative ways. You may think that some of these hacks are out of reach due to your time and resources, but don't assume that these activities and practices are impossible. Start with one hack, live with it for several days, and get teachers and students on board to go on the journey with you. The main thing is to get out of your comfort zone so you can learn and grow together.

These hacks will take time and support from your learning community, so begin sharing the ideas presented in the book with your administrators and teachers. Show your excitement, and it will create synergy in the building. This movement can change everything in your school.

Remember that the goal is to have a relevant program that makes a difference for your students and teachers. Try the hacks and share the results with your learning community and personal learning network. If you develop new hacks, be sure to share them on social media with your own network, and with ours, so other educators can learn from you. What are you waiting for? Start hacking your school library today! We would love to hear about the great things you are doing, so share on Twitter using #HackYourLibrary.

HACKING EDUCATION
10 Quick Fixes For Every School

By Mark Barnes (@markbarnes19) & Jennifer Gonzalez (@cultofpedagogy)

In the award-winning first Hack Learning Series book, *Hacking Education*, Mark Barnes and Jennifer Gonzalez employ decades of teaching experience and hundreds of discussions with education thought leaders to show you how to find and hone the quick fixes that every school and classroom need. Using a Hacker's mentality, they provide **one Aha moment after another** with 10 Quick Fixes For Every School—solutions to everyday problems and teaching methods that any teacher or administrator can implement immediately.

"Barnes and Gonzalez don't just solve problems; they turn teachers into hackers—a transformation that is right on time."

—Don Wettrick, Author of *Pure Genius*

HACKING PROJECT BASED LEARNING
10 Easy Steps to PBL and Inquiry in the Classroom
By Ross Cooper (@rosscoops31) and Erin Murphy (@murphysmusings5)

As questions and mysteries around PBL and inquiry continue to swirl, experienced classroom teachers and school administrators Ross Cooper and Erin Murphy have written a book that will empower those intimidated by PBL to cry, "I can do this!" while at the same time providing added value for those who are already familiar with the process. Impacting teachers and leaders around the world, *Hacking Project Based Learning* demystifies what PBL is all about with **10 hacks that construct a simple path** that educators and students can easily follow to achieve success. Forget your prior struggles with project based learning. This book makes PBL an amazing gift you can give all students tomorrow!

"*Hacking Project Based Learning* is a classroom essential. Its ten simple 'hacks' will guide you through the process of setting up a learning environment in which students will thrive from start to finish."

—Daniel H. Pink, *New York Times* Bestselling Author of *DRIVE*

HACKING ASSESSMENT
10 Ways To Go Gradeless In a Traditional Grades School
By Starr Sackstein (@mssackstein)

In the bestselling *Hacking Assessment,* award-winning teacher and world-renowned formative assessment expert Starr Sackstein unravels one of education's oldest mysteries: How to assess learning without grades—even in a school that uses numbers, letters, GPAs, and report cards. While many educators can only muse about the possibility of a world without grades, teachers like Sackstein are **reimagining education**. In this unique, eagerly-anticipated book, Sackstein shows you exactly how to create a remarkable no-grades classroom like hers, a vibrant place where students grow, share, thrive, and become independent learners who never ask, "What's this worth?"

"The beauty of the book is that it is not an empty argument against grades—but rather filled with valuable alternatives that are practical and will help to refocus the classroom on what matters most."

—ADAM BELLOW, WHITE HOUSE PRESIDENTIAL INNOVATION FELLOW

HACKING LEADERSHIP
10 Ways Great Leaders Inspire Learning That Teachers, Students, and Parents Love

By Joe Sanfelippo (@joe_sanfelippo) and Tony Sinanis (@tonysinanis)

In the runaway bestseller *Hacking Leadership*, internationally known school leaders Joe Sanfelippo and Tony Sinanis bring readers inside schools that few stakeholders have ever seen—places where students not only come first but have a unique voice in teaching and learning. Sanfelippo and Sinanis ignore the bureaucracy that stifles many leaders, focusing instead on building a culture of **engagement, transparency and, most important, fun**. *Hacking Leadership* has superintendents, principals, and teacher leaders around the world employing strategies they never before believed possible and learning how to lead from the middle. Want to revolutionize teaching and learning at your school or district? *Hacking Leadership* is your blueprint. Read it today, energize teachers and learners tomorrow!

"The authors do a beautiful job of helping leaders focus inward, instead of outward. This is an essential read for leaders who are, or want to lead, learner-centered schools."

—GEORGE COUROS, AUTHOR OF *THE INNOVATOR'S MINDSET*

HACKING SCHOOL CULTURE
Designing Compassionate Classrooms

By Angela Stockman (@angelastockman) and Ellen Feig Gray (@ellenfeiggray)

Bullying prevention and character-building programs are deepening our awareness of how today's kids struggle and how we might help, but many agree: They aren't enough to create school cultures where students and staff flourish. This inspired Angela Stockman and Ellen Feig Gray to begin seeking out systems and educators who were getting things right. Their experiences taught them that the **real game changers are using a human-centered approach**. Inspired by other design thinkers, many teachers are creating learning environments where seeking a greater understanding of themselves and others is the highest standard. They're also realizing that compassion is best cultivated in the classroom, not the boardroom or the auditorium. It's here that we learn how to pull one another close. It's here that we begin to negotiate the distances between us, too.

"*Hacking School Culture: Designing Compassionate Classrooms* is a valuable addition to the Hack Learning Series. It provides concrete support and suggestions for teachers to improve their interactions with their students at the same time they enrich their own professional experiences. Although primarily aimed at K–12 classrooms, the authors' insightful suggestions have given me, a veteran college professor, new insights into positive classroom dynamics which I have already begun to incorporate into my classes."

—LOUISE HAINLINE, PH.D., PROFESSOR OF PSYCHOLOGY, BROOKLYN COLLEGE OF CUNY

HACKING EARLY LEARNING
10 Building Blocks to Success in Pre-K–3 That All Teachers and School Leaders Should Know

By Jessica Cabeen (@jessicacabeen)

School readiness, closing achievement gaps, partnering with families, and innovative learning are just a few of the reasons the early learning years are the most critical years in a child's life. In what ways have schools lost the critical components of early learning—preschool through third grade—and how can we intentionally bring those ideas and instructional strategies back? In *Hacking Early Learning*, kindergarten school leader, early childhood education specialist, and Minnesota State Principal of the Year Jessica Cabeen provides strategies for teachers, principals, and district administrators for **best practices in preschool through third grade,** including connecting these strategies to all grade levels.

"Jessica Cabeen is not afraid to say she's learned from her mistakes and misconceptions. But it is those mistakes and misconceptions that qualify her to write this book, with its wonderfully user-friendly format. For each problem specified, there is a hack and actionable advice presented as "What You Can Do Tomorrow" and "A Blueprint for Full Implementation." Jessica's leadership is informed by both head and heart and, because of that, her wisdom will be of value to those who wish to teach and lead in the early childhood field."

—Rae Pica, Early Childhood Education Keynote Speaker
and Author of *What If Everybody Understood Child Development?*

HACKING ENGAGEMENT
50 Tips & Tools to Engage Teachers and Learners Daily
By James Alan Sturtevant (@jamessturtevant)

Some students hate your class. Others are just bored. Many are too nice, or too afraid, to say anything about it. Don't let it bother you; it happens to the best of us. But now, it's **time to engage!** In *Hacking Engagement*, the seventh book in the Hack Learning Series, veteran high school teacher, author, and popular podcaster James Sturtevant provides 50—that's right five-oh—tips and tools that will engage even the most reluctant learners daily. Sold in dozens of countries around the world, *Hacking Engagement* has become an educator's go-to guide for better student engagement in all grades and subjects. In fact, this book is so popular, Sturtevant penned a followup, *Hacking Engagement Again*, which brings 50 more powerful strategies. Find both at HackLearningBooks.com.

HACKING DIGITAL LEARNING STRATEGIES
10 Ways to Launch EdTech Missions in Your Classroom
By Shelly Sanchez Terrell
(@ShellTerrell)

In this breakthrough book, international EdTech presenter and NAPW Woman of the Year Shelly Sanchez Terrell demonstrates the power of EdTech Missions—lessons and projects that inspire learners to use web tools and social media to innovate, research, collaborate, problem-solve, campaign, crowd fund, crowdsource, and publish. The 10 Missions in *Hacking DLS* are more than enough to transform how teachers integrate technology, but there's also much more here. Included in the book is a **38-page Mission Toolkit**, complete with reproducible mission cards, badges, polls, and other handouts that you can copy and distribute to students immediately.

"The secret to Shelly's success as an education collaborator on a global scale is that she shares information most revered by all educators, information that is original, relevant, and vetted, combining technology with proven education methodology in the classroom. This book provides relevance to a 21st-century educator."

—THOMAS WHITBY, AUTHOR, PODCASTER, BLOGGER, CONSULTANT, CO-FOUNDER OF #EDCHAT

HACKING CLASSROOM MANAGEMENT

10 Ideas To Help You Become the Type of Teacher They Make Movies About

By Mike Roberts (@baldroberts)

Utah English Teacher of the Year and sought-after speaker Mike Roberts brings you 10 quick and easy classroom management hacks that will **make your classroom the place to be** for all your students. He shows you how to create an amazing learning environment that actually makes discipline, rules, and consequences obsolete, no matter if you're a new teacher or a 30-year veteran teacher.

"Mike writes from experience; he's learned, sometimes the hard way, what works and what doesn't, and he shares those lessons in this fine little book. The book is loaded with specific, easy-to-apply suggestions that will help any teacher create and maintain a classroom where students treat one another with respect, and where they learn."

—Chris Crowe, English Professor at BYU, Past President of ALAN, Author of *Death Coming Up the Hill, Getting Away with Murder: The True Story of the Emmett Till Case; Mississippi Trial, 1955*

HACKING THE WRITING WORKSHOP

Redesign with Making in Mind

*By Angela Stockman
(@AngelaStockman)*

Agility matters. This is what Angela Stockman learned when she left the classroom over a decade ago to begin supporting young writers and their teachers in schools. What she learned transformed her practice and led to the publication of her primer on this topic: *Make Writing: 5 Teaching Strategies that Turn Writer's Workshop Into a Maker Space.* Now, Angela is back with more stories from the road and **plenty of new thinking** to share. In *Make Writing,* Stockman upended the traditional writing workshop by combining it with the popular ideas that drive the maker space. Now, she is expanding her concepts and strategies and breaking new ground in *Hacking the Writing Workshop.*

"Good writing is good thinking. This is a book about how to think better, for yourself and with others."

—DAVE GRAY, FOUNDER OF XPLANE, AND AUTHOR OF *THE CONNECTED COMPANY, GAMESTORMING, AND LIMINAL THINKING*

The uN series

THE UNSERIES Teaching Reimagined

The uNseries is for teachers who love the uNlovable, accept the uNacceptable, rebuild the broken, and help the genius soar. Through each book in the uNseries, you will learn how to continue your growth as a teacher, leader, and influencer. The goal is that together we can become better than we ever could be alone. Each chapter uNveils an important principle to ponder, uNravels a plan that you can put into place to make an even greater impact, and uNleashes an action step for you to take to be a better educator. Learn more about the **uNseries and everything uN** at unseries.com.

uNforgettable
Your Roadmap to Being the Teacher They Never Forget
by Chuck Poole (@cpoole27)

"These 10 destinations will give you the inspiration and knowledge you need to take action and leave a lasting impression for years to come. Chuck Poole will be your guide. Through every twist and turn, you will be empowered, encouraged, and equipped to reimagine teaching in a way that will influence your students for a lifetime."

189

HACK LEARNING RESOURCES

SITES:

times10books.com
hacklearning.org
hacklearningbooks.com
unseries.com
teachonomy.com

PODCASTS:

hacklearningpodcast.com
jamesalansturtevant.com/podcast
teachonomy.com/podcast

FREE TOOLKIT FOR TEACHERS:

hacklearningtoolkit.com

ON TWITTER:

@HackMyLearning
#HackLearning
#HackLearningDaily
#WeTeachuN
#HackingLeadership
#HackingMath
#HackingLiteracy
#HackingEngagement
#HackingHomework

#HackingPBL
#MakeWriting
#EdTechMissions
#MovieTeacher
#HackingEarlyLearning
#CompassionateClassrooms
#HackGoogleEdu
#HackYourLibrary
#QuitPoint

HACK LEARNING ON FACEBOOK:

facebook.com/hacklearningseries

HACK LEARNING ON INSTAGRAM:

hackmylearning

MEET THE AUTHORS

Kristina A. Holzweiss is a certified school librarian, educational technology specialist, and secondary English teacher. She earned her Master's of Science in Library and Information Science (School Library Media) from the Palmer School of Library and Information Science at Long Island University, and holds certifications in school library media, educational technology, and English (7–12). Kristina was named the School Library Journal Librarian of the Year in 2015, a National School Board "20 to Watch" emerging education technology leader in 2017, and a Library Journal Mover & Shaker in 2018. Kristina is the president of the nonprofit organization Long Island LEADS (longislandleads.org), a community effort to learn, educate, advocate, develop, and support the maker movement and STEAM education (science, technology, engineering, art, and math). Long Island LEADS is a founding member of the Nation of Makers. In 2015, she founded SLIME—Students of Long Island Maker Expo (slimemakerexpo.com), an event where schools, libraries, museums, nonprofit organizations, civic associations, and educational companies can celebrate creativity and innovation. Previously she has co-written makerspace books for children with Scholastic. Kristina shares ideas and resources on her blog, bunheadwithducttape.com, and through Twitter and Instagram with the handle @lieberrian.

 Stony Evans is a teacher-librarian at Lakeside High School in Hot Springs, Arkansas. He earned his Master's in Library Media and Information Technologies from the University of Central Arkansas. Stony received the Arkansas Library Association's Retta Patrick Award in 2017, and was a finalist for the AASL 2017 Sensational Student Voice—Social Media Superstar award. He was selected as the Arkansas Association of Instructional Media's Library Media Specialist of the Year in 2013. He has been a school library advocacy columnist for *School Library Connection* magazine since 2015, and contributed a chapter to the book *Using Social Media to Build Library Communities: A LITA Guide*, in 2017. He is a Mackin TYSL Advocate, a Microsoft Innovative Educator Expert, and a Skype Master Teacher. Learn more about Stony by following him on Twitter @stony12270 or visiting librarymediatechtalk. blogspot.com.

ACKNOWLEDGMENTS

Kristina

My husband, Mike, has always believed in me, and is my inspiration for everything I do. My children, Tyler, Riley, and Lexy, have taught me so much about the importance of balancing family and my professional career. I hope that I am an example to them of what can happen through hard work and determination. A special thank you to Stony for joining me, and to all of my library friends who have inspired me on this wonderful learning journey.

Stony

I dedicate this book to my wife and best friend, Cindy, who has helped me at each step of the journey. Thank you, Kristina, for inviting me on this grand adventure of composing a book together. Also, many thanks to my Lakeside High School Library co-workers, Kaitlyn, Ray, and Peggy. I am also thankful to our administration and teachers for supporting our collaborations. It takes a village to create the library programming discussed in this publication.

X10

Vision, Experience, Action

Times 10 is helping all education stakeholders improve every aspect of teaching and learning. We are committed to solving big problems with simple ideas. We bring you content from experts, shared through multiple channels, including books, podcasts, and an array of social networks. Our mantra is simple: Read it today; fix it tomorrow. Stay in touch with us at Times10Books.com, at #HackLearning on Twitter, and on the Hack Learning Facebook page.

Made in the USA
San Bernardino, CA
31 May 2019